TO SETTLE THE SUCCESSION OF THE STATE

CONTEXT AND COMMENTARY

Series Editor: ARTHUR POLLARD

Published

J. A. V. Chapple
SCIENCE AND LITERATURE IN THE NINETEENTH
CENTURY

J. A. Downie
TO SETTLE THE SUCCESSION OF THE STATE

Dominic Hibberd
THE FIRST WORLD WAR

Pamela Horn
LIFE AND LABOUR IN RURAL ENGLAND,
1760–1850

Elisabeth Jay
FAITH AND DOUBT IN VICTORIAN BRITAIN

Norman Page
THE THIRTIES IN BRITAIN

Stephen Prickett
ENGLAND AND THE FRENCH REVOLUTION

Alan and Dorothy Shelston
THE INDUSTRIAL CITY

Robin Headlam Wells
SHAKESPEARE, POLITICS AND THE STATE

Forthcoming

Roger Richardson
REVOLT AND RESTORATION IN THE
SEVENTEENTH CENTURY

TO SETTLE THE SUCCESSION OF THE STATE

Literature and Politics, 1678–1750

J. A. Downie

MACMILLAN

First published 1994 by
THE MACMILLAN PRESS LTD
Houndmills, Basingstoke, Hampshire RG21 2XS
and London
Companies and representatives
throughout the world

ISBN 0–333–49596–9 hardcover
ISBN 0–333–49597–7 paperback

A catalogue record for this book is available
from the British Library

Printed in Hong Kong

For Jemima

Contents

Acknowledgements   viii
Note on the Texts   ix
Editor's Preface   xi

Introduction   1

1. The Popish Plot and the Exclusion Crisis   5

2. Revolution and Revolution Settlement   31

3. The Rage of Party   63

4. Public Virtues, Private Vices   90

5. The Opposition to Walpole   111

Epilogue: The Forty-Five   146

Notes   157
Chronological Table   158
Bibliography   162
Index   166

Acknowledgements

I should like to thank Elizabeth Horsley, Tim Parnell, and Bill Speck for reading portions of the manuscript in draft, and for making a number of valuable suggestions.

Note on the Texts

As this is a volume in the 'Context and Commentary' series, all quotations are from the original editions – the first edition unless otherwise indicated – and largely follow contemporary typographical practice with regard to spelling, punctuation, capitalisation, and italicisation. I have, however, abandoned the use of the long **s**, as well as silently correcting obvious misprints. Any other alterations from the original editions are indicated by the use of square brackets.

Editor's Preface

J. H. Plumb has said that 'the aim of (the historian) is to understand men both as individuals and in their social relationships in time. "Social" embraces all of man's activities – economic, religious, political, artistic, legal, military, scientific – everything, indeed, that affects the life of mankind.' Literature is itself similarly comprehensive. From Terence onwards writers have embraced his dictum that all things human are their concern.

It is the aim of this series to trace the interweavings of history and literature, to show by judicious quotation and commentary how those actually working within the various fields of human activity influenced and were influenced by those who were writing the novels, poems and plays within the several periods. An attempt has been made to show the special contribution that such writers make to the understanding of their times by virtue of their peculiar imaginative 'feel' for their subjects and the intensely personal angle from which they observe the historical phenomena that provide their inspiration and come within their creative vision. In its turn the historical evidence, besides and beyond its intrinsic importance, serves to 'place' the imaginative testimony of the writers.

The authors of the several volumes in this series have sought to intermingle history and literature in the conviction that the study of each is enhanced thereby. They have been free to adopt their own approach within the broad general pattern of the series. The topics themselves have sometimes also a particular slant and emphasis. Commentary, for instance, has had to be more detailed in some cases than in others. All the contributors to the series are at one, however, in the belief (at a time when some critics would not only divorce texts from their periods but even from their authors) that literature is the creation of actual men and women, actually living in an identifiable set of historical circumstances, themselves both the creatures and the creators of their times.

ARTHUR POLLARD

ALL humane things are subject to decay,
And when Fate Summons, Monarch's must obey;
This *Flecknoe* found, who like *Augustus* young,
Was call'd to Empire, and had Govern'd long;
In Prose and Verse was own'd without Dispute,
Through all the Realms of Nonsense, Absolute;
This Aged Prince now flourishing in Peace,
And blest with Issue of a large Increase,
Worn out with Business, did at length Debate,
To settle the Succession of the State....

John Dryden, *Mac Flecknoe* (1682), p. 3

Introduction

Cease then, nor ORDER Imperfection name:
Our proper bliss depends on what we blame.
Know thy own point: This kind, this due degree
Of blindness, weakness, Heav'n bestows on thee.
Submit—In this, or any other sphere,
Secure to be as blest as thou canst bear:
Safe in the hand of one disposing Pow'r,
Or in the natal, or the mortal hour.
All Nature is but Art, unknown to thee;
All Chance, Direction, which thou canst not see;
All Discord, Harmony, not understood;
All partial Evil, universal Good:
And, spite of Pride, in erring Reason's spite,
One truth is clear, 'Whatever IS, is RIGHT.'

Alexander Pope, *An Essay on Man* (1743), pp. 25–7

The relationship of literature and history is more complicated than critics and historians either used to realise, or were prepared to acknowledge. In the era of the New Criticism, indeed, students of literature were encouraged simply to ignore historical background when interpreting the text, even though, as Wayne C. Booth later remarked, that 'all literary interpretation is [...] dependent on history should have been obvious to everyone' (*A Rhetoric of Irony*, p. 132*n*). Other objectors to the relevance of historical context argued 'that the meanings of the past are intrinsically alien to us, that we have no "authentic" access to those meanings and therefore can never "truly" understand them' (E. D. Hirsch, *Validity in Interpretation*, p. 40). More recently, deconstruction has once again drawn attention to the problems attending those who wish to bring historical information to bear on the task of interpretation. Historians, on the other hand, have often been reluctant even to address the methodological issues surrounding the use of literary evidence, and have tended to content themselves with the anecdotal, plundering novels or plays for juicy quotations, and so on. But before they can mean anything at all, sources have to be interpreted. This applies to all sources, not just works of literature. Hermeneutical issues should be at the cutting edge of debates between historians, but more often than not, they, too, seem simply to be ignored.

Leaving more complex issues of reading and interpretation to one side for the moment, it would appear to be indisputable that there was, in England, a close correlation between literature and topical politics in the period between the Popish Plot and the Forty-Five rebellion. In many works of the period currently studied at sixth-form or undergraduate level, political context is necessary if the reader is to understand what is going on even at a fairly basic level. This was, after all, what has been described as the 'First Age of Party', when politics infected not only the hustings and Westminster Hall, but the church, the coffee-house, and the drawing-room. The first political parties emerged in response to grave misgivings about who should succeed Charles II on the throne of England, and for the next seventy years English politics was dominated to such an extent by the question of the succession that all other issues might be said to be at least related to it, if not subsumed into it.

Paradoxically, party politics is perhaps not the most interesting feature of the political literature of the period. Just so long as they belonged to the privileged elite, there was a great deal of common ground between the vast majority of Whigs and Tories. Their battles were more like disputes between present-day Democrats and Republicans in the United States than the expression of fundamentally different ways of viewing the world such as that between capitalism and socialism. Most Whigs and Tories were massively conservative and shared an ideology of order and hierarchy. Apart from a majority of the Dissenters and the handful of Whigs who seriously entertained notions of a democratic nature, the common objective of the politics of the propertied members of each party was to perpetuate their privileged position in society. 'Now, tho' the Opinions of both these [parties] are very consistent, and I really think are maintain'd at present by a great Majority of the Kingdom', wrote Swift in 1711, 'yet, according as Men apprehend the Danger greater, either from the *Pretender* and his Party, or from the

Violence and Cunning of *other Enemies* to the Constitution; so their common Discourses and Reasonings, turn either to the first or second Set of these Opinions I have mention'd, and are consequently styl'd either *Whigs* or *Tories*' (*The Examiner* No. 44: 24–31 May 1711).

In reality, there was, as we shall see, more to disputes between Whig and Tory than this, but Swift's point is an important one which it is crucial not to forget. Beyond the topicalities of party politics, more fundamental questions were being posed relating to the nature of man, the structure of society, the origins and purpose of government, and the existence (or non-existence) of God. The principal justification for a hierarchical society, in which most of the power and wealth was to be located in the hands of a few men, was religious. It was based on Scripture, and in particular on the Ten Commandments and other biblical injunctions against insubordination. To understand the context of 'Augustan' literature, it is necessary to try to identify the ideological underpinning of society in 'Augustan' England. What Augustan literature appears to illustrate, above all, is that morality is an ideological construct. The Augustan satirists were greatly concerned about morality, but they were merely following the lead provided by contemporary political philosophers and controversialists. Algernon Sidney supplied what is perhaps the most succinct contemporary statement linking ideology with social behaviour: 'Liberty cannot be preserv'd, if the manners of the People are corrupted' (*Discourses concerning Government* (1704), p. 180). The lower orders had to be kept in their place if the status quo was to be maintained.

One means of achieving this was to publish writings which promulgated one way of looking at the world rather than another. These were not simply targeted at the lower orders, although *The Whole Duty of Man* was addressed to the 'meanest readers'. *The Tatler* made no apology for offering 'something, whereby [...] worthy and well-affected Members of the Commonwealth may be instructed, after their Reading, *what to think*' (*The Tatler* No. 1: 12 April 1709). By studying Augustan literature in its political context, we can begin to appreciate the subtle ways in which literature not merely reflects ideology, but in fact confirms or modifies it. In this context, the term 'ideology' is not meant to carry any of the pejorative associations it has been accorded by modern politicians of a conservative persuasion. A useful synonym for our purposes might be the German word, *Weltanschauung*, which roughly translates as 'world-picture' or 'world-view'. An ideology is most pervasive when it is not even acknowledged to be an ideology, but is regarded simply as 'reality' or 'the way things are'. A society's unspoken assumptions are very often the most useful keys to understanding its customs or social conventions.

By 'ideology' therefore is meant what has been called 'the set of reflections and refractions of social and natural reality that is held by the human brain and which the brain expresses and fixes through words, drawings, lines, or whatever signifying form' (Todorov, *Mikhail Bakhtin: The Dialogical Principle* (1984), p. 18), and in this case we shall be concentrating on the 'signifying form' of the printed word.

Finally, it should be pointed out that I have made a conscious decision *not* to distinguish between so-called 'literary' texts and 'non-literary' texts, nor to privilege what are sometimes referred to as 'works of the creative imagination'. Although I have no intention of neglecting classic passages from well-known texts just because they are well-known, and therefore readily available elsewhere, I have tried to introduce passages from texts which are not usually quoted either by critics or historians. It can, I think, be quite effective to present the unusual and the well-known in juxtaposition, and thus I have alternated references to, and quotations from, famous writers, and from those who are not so famous.

1 The Popish Plot and the Exclusion Crisis

From hence began that Plot, the Nation's Curse,
Bad in it self, but represented worse.
Rais'd in extremes, and in extremes decry'd;
With Oaths affirm'd, with dying Vows deny'd.
Not weigh'd, or winnow'd by the Multitude;
But swallow'd in the Mass, unchew'd and Crude.
Some Truth there was, but dash'd and brew'd with Lyes;
To please the Fools, and puzzle all the Wise.
Succeeding times did equal folly call,
Believing nothing, or believing all [. . . .]

John Dryden, *Absalom and Achitophel* (1681), pp. 4–5

On 13 August 1678 Charles II was informed of a plot against his life. The details were supplied by a discredited Jesuit novice called Titus Oates, who gave an account of a resolution, taken at a meeting of Jesuits held in London, to kill the King 'by shooting, stabbing, or poisoning'. Now rumours of assassination plots were commonplace, but it was an offence (misprison) to withhold evidence of treason and, as Charles himself later explained to Gilbert Burnet, 'among so many particulars he did not know but there might be some truth' (*History of My Own Time*, II, 149).

Nevertheless, six weeks elapsed before Oates was examined by the Privy Council. Even though he insisted on taking an oath, it was suspected that Oates was making up most, if not all, of his story. While the investigations into his accusations were still going on, however, he had the first of two extraordinary strokes of luck. Prior to coming before the Council, he had made a series of depositions before a Justice of the Peace. On 17 October, the body of the Justice, Sir Edmund Berry Godfrey, was found at the bottom of a ditch. Naturally enough, given the sensational aspects of Oates' account, details of Privy Council proceedings had been circulating. The temptation to put two and two together was overwhelming. Godfrey had been murdered by the Papists! Within a week, Parliament had reassembled and Oates had been called before the Bar of the House of Commons.

At this point Oates had his second piece of good fortune when one of his random accusations actually struck home. In the course of its investigations the Privy Council had ordered the seizing of the papers of several of the prominent Catholics mentioned by name by Oates in the course of his interrogation. Those of the Duke of York's secretary, Edward Coleman, revealed that Coleman had indeed been involved in a plot of some kind to overthrow the Church of England and re-establish Roman Catholicism as the national faith. On 31 October a number of Coleman's letters were read to the Commons, upon which a resolution was passed: 'That, upon the Evidence that has already appeared to this House, That this House is of Opinion, that there hath been, and still is, a damnable and hellish Plot contrived and carried on by the Popish Recusants, for the Assassinating and Murdering the King; and for subverting the Government; and rooting out and destroying the Protestant Religion' (*Journals of the House of Commons*, IX, 530).

Once the existence of a Popish Plot had been given this official countenance, the question of the safety of the Protestant succession became a matter of national urgency. As Charles II had no legitimate offspring, the next in line to the throne was his brother, James, Duke of York, the very man whose secretary had just become entangled in Oates' web of intrigue. Worse, James was himself a Roman Catholic. On 9 November in an address to both Houses of Parliament Charles agreed in principle to provisions for individual and national security during the reign of any Catholic successor 'so as they tend not to impeach the Right of Succession, nor the Descent of the Crown in the true Line' (*Journals of the House of Commons*, IX, 536). Such assurances notwithstanding, it did not take very long before it was being openly suggested that the Duke of York should simply be excluded from the line of succession.

Popery had long been associated with arbitrary government in the minds of the majority of Englishmen. John Foxe's *Acts and Monuments* – more usually referred to as Foxe's Book of Martyrs – kept alive the old stories of Catholic persecution of Protestants under Bloody Mary, and to this was added the memory of the

Gunpowder Plot, as well as of more recent 'Popish' outrages. Even the Fire of London was linked with Popery in the popular imagination. Of still greater significance the events of the 1640s were a constant reminder not only of the consequences of civil war but of a supposed earlier plot 'to alter the kingdom both in religion and government'. Had there not been a long tradition to draw on, the reaction to Oates' revelations would not have been so extreme. 'To suppose that Oates's so-called discoveries were a monstrous concoction which deprived the nation of its senses at one stroke is misleading and can only create a distorted picture of the crisis as a whole', J. R. Jones sagely observes, 'Oates's stories had such an effect because they appealed on different levels to every section of the nation, they confirmed assumptions about the Papists held by almost everyone, and they were coupled with the fear of absolutism and slavery' (*The First Whigs* (1961), p. 21).

Before long the nation seemed to be divided into two camps or parties: those who supported Exclusion and those to whom the idea was anathema. The latter, the King's party, became distinguished by the name of Tories, 'a Name of Contempt given them by their Adversaries, from the Robbers in Ireland so call'd' (*Tories and Tory Principles Ruinous to both Prince and People* (1714), p. 19). The former, the Exclusionists, had already been derisively labelled Whigs in allusion to the fanatically anti-Catholic Scottish whiggamores, later graphically portrayed by Sir Walter Scott in his novel *Old Mortality*. Pre-eminent amongst the Exclusionists was the Earl of Shaftesbury, the undisputed leader of the Opposition not only within Parliament but also in the nation at large, as Dryden's malicious portrait of him as the 'ungrateful' Achitophel makes abundantly clear:

> Of these the false Achitophel was first,
> A Name to all succeeding Ages Curst:
> For close Designs, and crooked Counsell fit;
> Sagacious, Bold, and Turbulent of wit:
> Restless, unfixt in Principle and Place;
> In Power unpleas'd, impatient of Disgrace.
> A fiery Soul, which working out its way,
> Fretted the Pigmy Body to decay:
> And o'r inform'd the Tenement of Clay.
> A daring Pilot in extremity;

Pleas'd with the Danger, when the Waves went high
He sought the Storms; but, for a Calm unfit,
Would Steer too nigh the Sands, to boast his Wit.
Great Wits are sure to Madness near ally'd;
And thin Partitions do their Bounds divide:
Else why should he, with Wealth and Honour blest,
Refuse his Age the needful hours of Rest?
Punish a Body which he coud not please;
Bankrupt of Life, yet Prodigal of Ease?
And all to leave, what with his Toyl he won,
To that unfeather'd, two Leg'd thing, a Son:
Got, while his Soul did hudled Notions try;
And born a shapeless Lump, like Anarchy.
In Friendship False, Implacable in Hate:
Resolv'd to Ruin, or to Rule the State.

John Dryden, *Absalom and Achitophel* (1681), p. 6

Although to a modern reader it might seem reasonable to assume that Exclusion was indeed the readiest and easiest expedient to circumvent the possible consequences of a Popish Plot, as far as contemporaries were concerned the question of the succession went to the very heart of an ideological struggle which had been going on at least since the reign of Elizabeth I. In Shakespeare's play Richard II is portrayed as a bad king who governs without regard to the national interest. Nevertheless, the Bishop of Carlisle argues, Richard is not answerable to his subjects:

And shall the figure of Gods Majesty,
His Captaine, steward, deputy, elect,
Annointed, crowned, planted, many yeares
Be iudg'd by subject and inferiour breath,
And he himselfe not present? Oh forfend it God [. . . .]

William Shakespeare, *Richard II* (1597), p. H^r

The early Stuart clergy had made it their business to establish the orthodoxy that kings not only derived their power from God alone but were His divinely-anointed lieutenants upon earth. That such ideas remained current during the reign of Charles II is made perfectly clear by an address presented to the King by the University of Cambridge in 1681:

> We will still believe and maintain, That our Kings derive not their Titles from the People, but from God; that to him only they are accountable; that it belongs not to Subjects, either to cieate or censure, but to honor and obey their Sovereign, who comes to be so by a fundamental hereditary Right of Succession, which no Religion, no Law, no Fault or Forfeiture can alter or diminish.
>
> Abednigo Seller, *The History of Passive Obedience Since the Reformation* (1689), p. 108

If this were so, then the succession could not simply be altered to suit the wishes of the people.

Indefeasible hereditary right, passive obedience and non-resistance were integral components of the doctrine which is traditionally (if not entirely accurately) referred to as 'the Divine Right of Kings'. James I himself outlined the theory of royal absolutism which underpinned Divine Right. 'In the Scriptures Kings are called Gods', he explained in 1610 in a speech to Parliament. 'Kings are also compared to Fathers of families: for a King is trewly *Parens patriæ*, the politique father of his people' (James I, *Workes* (1616), p. 529). It was in accordance with thinking such as this that the biblical injunction, 'Honour thy father, and thy mother', was extended to the civil powers, as that Restoration best-seller, *The Whole Duty of Man*, took pains to explain:

> 1. The *first* of those neerer sorts of relations, is that of a *Parent*; And here it will be necessary to consider the severall sorts of *Parents*, according to which the duty of them is to be measured. Those are these three, the *Civil*, the *Spiritual*, the *Natural*.
>
> 2. The *Civil Parent* is he, whom God hath establisht the *Supreme Magistrate*, who by a just right possesses the throne in a Nation. This is the common Father of all those that are under his authority. The duty we owe to this *Parent* is, *first*, *Honour* and *Reverence*, looking on him,

as upon one, on whom God hath stamped much of his own power and authority, and therefore paying him all honour and esteem, never daring, upon any pretence whatsoever, to *speak evil of the ruler of our people*, Acts 23. 5.

3. *Secondly*, Paying *Tribute*; This is expressly commanded by the Apostle, *Rom.* 13. 6. *Pay ye tribute also, for they are Gods Ministers attending continually upon this very thing.* God has set them apart as Ministers for the common good of the people, and therefore 'tis all justice, they should be maintained and supported by them. And indeed when it is considered, what are the cares; and troubles of that high calling, how many thorns are platted in every Crown, we have very little reason to envy them these dues, and it may truly be said, there is none of their poor labouring subjects, that earns their living so hardly.

4. *Thirdly*, We are to pray for them: this is also expressly commanded by the Apostle, I. *Tim.* 2. 2. to be done for Kings, *and for all that are in authority.* The business of that calling are [*sic*] so weighty, the dangers and hazards of it so great, that they of all others need prayers for Gods direction, assistance, and blessing, and the prayers that are thus poured out for them, will return into our own bosomes, for the blessings they receive from God tend to the good of the people, to their *living a quiet and peaceable life*, as it is in the close of the verse forementioned.

5. *Fourthly*, We are to pay them *Obedience*. This is likewise strictly charged by the Apostle, I *Pet.* 2. 13. *Submit your selves to every ordinance of man for the Lords sake, whether it is to the King as Supreme, or unto Governours as those that are sent by him*; We owe such an *obedience* to the supreme power, that whoever is authorised by him, we are to submit to, and St. *Paul* likewise is most full to this purpose, *Rom.* 13. I. *Let every soul be subject to the higher powers*; and again, ver. 2. *Whosoever resisteth the powers, resisteth the Ordinance of God.* And 'tis observable that these precepts were given at a time, when those powers were Heathens, and cruel persecutors of Christianity, to shew us, that no pretence of the wickedness of our rulers, can free us of this duty. An *obedience* we must pay either

Active or Passive: the active in the case of all lawful commands; That is, when ever the Magistrate commands something, which is not contrary to some Command of God, we are then bound to act according to that command of the Magistrate, to do the thing he requires. But when he injoyns any thing contrary to what God hath commanded, we are not then to pay him this active *obedience*, we may, nay we must refuse thus to act, (yet here we must be very well assured that the thing is so contrary, and not pretend conscience for a cloak of stubbornness) we owe in that case to *obey God rather then man*. But even this is a season for the Passive obedience, we must patiently suffer, what he inflicts on us, for such refusal, and not, to secure our selves, rise up against him. For who can stretch his hand *against the Lords anointed, and be guiltless?* says *David* to *Abishai*, I *Sam.* 26. 9. and that at a time when *David* was under a great persecution from *Saul*, nay, had also the assurance of the Kingdom after him; and St. *Pauls* sentence in this case is most heavy. *Rom.* 13. 2. *They that resist shall receive to themselves damnation.* Here is very small incouragement to any to rise up against the lawful Magistrate, for though they should so far prosper here, as to secure themselves from him by this means, yet there is a King of kings, from whom no power can shelter him, and this damnation in the close will prove a sad prize of their victories.

Richard Allestree, *The Whole Duty of Man*
(1659), pp. 278–81

However, the simple fact that religious writers and clergymen felt it necessary to stress the teaching of Romans 13 – that submission to the powers that be is the fundamental duty of every Christian – is an indication of the pressures to which Divine Right theory was being subjected. Questions of authority and allegiance had been posed in their starkest form between 1640 and 1660, more especially after the execution of Charles I in 1649. In the aftermath of civil war, the question of political stability was high on the national agenda. There were good reasons for championing absolutism in Charles II's reign. As the Marquis of Halifax pointed out, 'he who practiseth disobedience to his superiors, teacheth it to his inferiors'. The propertied – those, in other words, who exercised political power – had a vested interest in guaranteeing the hierarchical structure of society. They were, accordingly, suspicious of the unpropertied masses, subscribing to them dangerous, democratic tendencies which, in turn, were usually regarded as anarchical in spirit, if not in fact.

This was Dryden's principal ploy in *Absalom and Achitophel*. 'I will not say who started the Game', Shaftesbury is reputed to have remarked about the Popish Plot, 'but I am sure I had the full hunting of it'. It was then only a short step to take to accuse Shaftesbury of fomenting rebellion:

> *Achitophel*, grown weary to possess
> A lawfull fame, and lazy Happiness;
> Disdain'd the Golden fruit to gather free,
> And lent the Croud his Arm to shake the Tree.
> Now, manifest of Crimes, contriv'd long since,
> He stood at bold Defiance with his Prince:
> Held up the Buckler of the Peoples Cause,
> Against the Crown; and sculk'd behind the Laws.
> The wish'd occasion of the Plot he takes,
> Some Circumstances finds, but more he makes.
> By buzzing Emissaries, fills the ears
> Of listning Crowds, with Jealosies and Fears
> Of Arbitrary Counsels brought to light,
> And proves the King himself a *Jebusite*:[1]
> Weak Arguments! which yet he knew ful well,
> Were strong with People easie to Rebell.

John Dryden, *Absalom and Achitophel* (1681), p. 7

Dryden was not alone in playing on the fears of the conservative elite, distorting the ideological position of the Opposition by dwelling on the supposed 'levelling' tendencies of the Exclusionists. In terms reminiscent of Rochester's notorious *Satyr against Reason and Mankind* (which first appeared in print in a broadside version in the same year, 1679) John Oldham in one of his *Satires upon the Jesuits* suggested that the Popish Plot itself was part of a much larger plan to overthrow not only the Protestant religion, but the existing social structure. In *Garnets Ghost* the Ghost of the Gunpowder plotter, Henry Garnet, addresses the Jesuits who are 'met in private Caball, just after the Murther of Sir Edmund-Bury Godfrey':

> Let rabble souls of narrow aim and reach;
> Stoop their vile necks, and dull Obedience preach.
> Let them with slavish awe, disdain'd by me:
> Adore the purple Rag of Majesty,
> And think't a sacred Relick of the sky.
> Well may such fools by subject to controul;
> To every Scepter'd Wretch that dares but rule:
> Unlike the soul with which, proud I was born;
> Who could that sneaking thing, a *Monarch* scorn;
> Spurn off a Crown, and set my foot in sport,
> Upon the head that wore it, trod in dirt.
> But say, what i'st that binds your hands? does fear,
> From such a glorious action, you deter?
> Or i'st Religion? but you sure disclaim
> That frivolous pretence, that empty Name:
> Meer bugbear word, devis'd by us to scare
> The senceless rout to slavishness and fear,
> Nere known to awe the brave, and those that dare.
> Such weak, and feeble things may serve for checks,
> To reign and curb base mettl'd *Hereticks*:
> Dull creatures, whose nice bogling consciences,
> Startle, or strain at such like crimes as these.
> Such whom fond inbred honesty befools;
> Or their old musty peice the Bible Gulls.
> That hated book, the Bullwark of our foes,
> Whereby they still uphold their tott'ring cause.

John Oldham, *Garnets Ghost* (1679) p. 2

In this way Oldham contrived to link several of the key issues in Restoration politics with the Popish Plot: was monarchy divinely-appointed or was it a man-made institution? were men bound by God to obedience to those in positions of authority or was this merely a means of social control? was there indeed a God able to punish those who transgressed His law or was religion itself simply an 'empty name' intended to maintain order, as Hobbes had pointed out with regard to 'the Religion of the Heathen'?

> And therefore the first Founders, and Legislators of Common-wealths amongst the Gentiles, whose ends were only to keep the people in obedience, and peace, have in all places taken care [...] to imprint in their minds a beliefe, that those precepts which they gave concerning Religion, might not be thought to proceed from their own device, but from the dictates of some God, or other Spirit.
>
> Thomas Hobbes, *Leviathan* (1651), p. 57

What Hobbes had written about heathen religions was quickly taken up by sceptics after the Restoration and applied to Christianity itself. To men of a conservative disposition, it was as if the very foundations of the world in which they had been brought up were being threatened during the years of the Popish Plot and the Exclusion Crisis, while rakes like the Earl of Rochester railed at the 'False freedoms, holy cheats, and formal lies' which had been invented in order to allow 'the pretending part of the proud world [...] Over their fellow slaves to tyrannize'. How else could the impiety of the *Satyr against Reason and Mankind* be interpreted?

> [...] thoughts are giv'n for Actions Government,
> Where Action ceases, thoughts impertinent:
> Our Sphere of Action, is lifes happiness,
> And he who thinks beyond, thinks like an Ass.
> Thus, whilst Against false reas'ning I inveigh,
> I own right Reason, which I wou'd obey:
> That Reason that distinguishes by sense
> And gives us Rules of good and bad from thence:
> That bounds desires, with a reforming will,
> To keep 'em more in vigour, not to kill.
>
> John Wilmot, Earl of Rochester, *Poems on Several Occasions* (1685), p. 9

The extent to which the thoughts of Englishmen were dislocated by the events of these years might be measured by the success in the winter of 1681–82 of Thomas Otway's tragedy, *Venice Preserved, or, A Plot Discover'd*, which set out, quite deliberately, to play upon contemporary fears of conspiracy in these 'distracted times when each man dreads/The bloudy stratagems of busie heads;/When we have fear'd three years we know not what'. Although conflicting signals make it difficult to discern a particularised political allegory, Otway's play apparently sets out to dramatise the clash of loyalties – and the clash of ideologies – with which many contemporaries were faced.

In *Venice Preserved* a decaying state and corrupt senators are challenged by a set of conspirators whose internecine quarrels and uncertainty about the rectitude of what they are about to attempt lead to unconvincing comparisons with the acts of Roman worthies. Tradition has it that in the person of the unscrupulous, self-seeking Renault, who insists that he is acting patriotically 'To prop the reeling glory of his country', Otway is satirising the Earl of Shaftesbury. What is not in doubt is the way in which *Venice Preserved* pointedly comments on the confused moralities of Restoration England:

> [*Bedamore*] Once more embrace, my Friends – wee'l all embrace – United thus, we are the mighty Engin Must twist this rooted Empire from its Basis! Totters it not already?
> *Eliot.* Would it were tumbling.
> *Bed.* Nay it shall down: This Night we Seal its ruine.
>
> *Enter* Pierre.
>
> Oh *Pierre*! thou art welcome!
> Come to my breast, for by its hopes thou look'st
> Lovelily dreadful, and the Fate of *Venice*
> Seems on thy Sword already. Oh my *Mars!*
> The Poets that first feign'd a God of War
> Sure prophesy'd of thee.
> *Pierr.* Friends! was not *Brutus*,
> (I mean that *Brutus*, who in open Senate
> Stabb'd the first *Cæsar* that usurp'd the World)
> A Gallant Man?
> *Rena.* Yes, and *Cateline* too;
> Tho story wrong his Fame: for he conspir'd
> To prop the reeling Glory of his Country:
> His Cause was good.

Beda. And ours as much above it,
As *Renault* thou art Superior to *Cethegus.*
Or *Pierre* to *Cassius.*
Pierr. Then to what we aim at
When do we start? or must we talk for ever?
Beda. No *Pierre,* the Deed's near Birth: Fate seems
    to have set
The Business up, and given it to our care,
I hope there's not a heart nor hand amongst us
But is firm and ready.
All. All!
Wee'l die with *Bedamore.*
Beda. O Men,
Matchless, as will your Glory be hereafter.
The Game is for a Matchless Prize, if won;
If lost, disgraceful Ruine.
Ren. What can lose it?
The publick Stock's a Beggar; one *Venetian*
Trusts not another: Look into their Stores
Of general safety; Empty Magazines,
A tatter'd Fleet, a murmuring unpaid Army,
Bankrupt Nobility, a harrast Commonalty,
A Factious, giddy, and divided Senate,
Is all the strength of *Venice*: Let's destroy it;
Let's fill their Magazines with Arms to awe them,
Man out their Fleet, and make their Trade maintain
    it;
Let loose the murmuring Army on their Masters,
To pay themselves with plunder; Lop their Nobles
To the base Roots, whence most of 'em first sprung;
Enslave the Rowt, whom smarting will make
    humble,
Turn out their droning Senate, and possess
That Seat of Empire which our Souls were fram'd
    for.
Pierr. Ten thousand men are Armed at your Nod,
Commanded all by Leaders fit to guide
A Battle for the freedom of the World;
This wretched State has starv'd them in its service,
And by your bounty quicken'd, they're resolv'd
To serve your Glory, and revenge their own!

Th' have all their different Quarters in this City,
Watch for th' Alarm, and grumble 'tis so tardy.
Beda. I doubt not Friend, but thy unweary'd
    diligence
Has still kept waking, and it shall have ease;
After this Night it is resolv'd we meet
Nomore, 'till *Venice* own us for her Lords.
Pierr. How lovely the *Adriatique* Whore,
Drest in her Flames, will shine! devouring Flames!
Such as shall burn her to the watery bott[o]m
And hiss in her Foundation.

> Thomas Otway, *Venice Preserved, or, A Plot*
> *Discover'd* (1682), pp. 19–21

Are these conspirators to be admired, or reviled? Even the terms in which the dialogue is couched are double-edged, as open talk of treason, usurpation, and conspiracy is balanced by Bedamore's insistence that we are watching men of 'high call-ing,/Men separated by the Choice of Providence,/From the gross heap of Mankind'. In this way the older ideology, which professed to recognise a divine order in the universe, is juxta-posed with the uncomfortable proposition that the conspirators who seek to overthrow the tottering state are somehow the agents of an inscrutable Providence. By making Pierre refer to the plot to overthrow the Senate as a 'Battle for the freedom of the World', Otway succeeds in alluding, however sarcastically, to the grander claims of the Exclusionists and their insistence that the safety of the Protestant succession and the protection of liberty and property were inextricably linked, and indeed *Venice Preserved* 'became an eighteenth-century emblem for "libertarian" sentiment, with Pierre as the hero' (Hume, 'Texts Within Con-texts', p. 86).

Interpretation of *Venice Preserved* is not made any easier by the fact that, ostensibly at least, Otway's play is about a republic and not a monarchy. It is, then, at least conceivable that Otway was consciously contributing to the contemporary debate about the nature and origins of government which had been going on throughout the seventeenth century, because not everyone was prepared to accept the doctrines of the Divine Right theorists. In the very month that Charles II was first informed about the existence of Titus Oates, the second edition of a most influential pamphlet by Andrew Marvell was posthumously published. The opening sentence stated Marvell's thesis most forcibly:

> THere has now for divers Years, a Design been carried on, to change the Lawful Government of *England* into an Absolute Tyranny, and to Convert the Established *Protestant Religion* into down-right *Popery*: than both which, nothing can be more Destructive or contrary to the Interest and Happiness, to the Constitution and Being of the King and Kingdom.
>
> Andrew Marvell, *An Account Of the Growth of Popery, And Arbitrary Government in England* (1678), pp. 3–4

Nowadays Marvell is known chiefly as a late practitioner of 'metaphysical' wit and the author of a handful of exquisite poems in that vein. His reputation amongst his contemporaries was very different, however. As MP for Hull Marvell was an outspoken critic of government policy. Until his *Miscellaneous Poems* appeared after his death in 1681 Marvell's fame rested on his verse satires on the court of Charles II, and still more on his skill as a controversialist in prose.

As well as offering a stark indication of the depth of anti-Catholic feeling in England in the autumn of 1678 upon which Oates and his accomplices were able to rely, *An Account Of the Growth of Popery* is at once characteristic of its era in assuming a connection between Popery and tyranny, and seminal in the arguments it adduces in support of its thesis. England was out of step with other seventeenth-century European countries in a number of ways. Increasingly continental monarchies, both Catholic and Protestant, were tending to move towards absolutism and arbitrary power. While he professed to discern a similar tendency in his own country, Marvell was at pains to spell out what he saw as the fundamental differences between England and other European monarchies:

> For if we first consider the State, the Kings of *England* Rule not upon the same terms with those of our Neighbour Nations, who, having by Force or by Address Usurped that due share which there [*sic*] People had in

the Government, are now for some Ages in possession of an Arbitrary Power (which yet no Prescription can make Legal) and Exercise it over their Persons and Estates in a most Tyrannical manner. But here the Subjects retain their proportion in the Legislature; the very meanest Commoner of *England* is represented in *Parliament*, and is a party to those Laws by which the Prince is Sworn to Govern himself and his People. No Money is to be Levied but by the common consent. No man is for *Life, Limb, Goods, or Liberty* at the Sovereigns Discretion: But we have the same Right (modestly understood) *in our Propriety* that the Prince hath *in his Regality*; and in all Cases where the King is concerned, we have our just Remedy as against any private Person of the Neighbour-hood, in the Courts of *Westminster-Hall*, or in the High Court of *Parliament*. His very Prerogative is no more than what the Law has determined. His Broad Seal, which is the Legitimate Stamp of his Pleasure, yet is no longer currant, than upon the Tryal it is found to be Legal. He cannot commit any Persons by his particular Warrant. He cannot himself be Witness in any Cause: The Balance of Publick Justice being so delicate, that not the head only, but even the breath of the Prince would turn the Scale. Nothing is left to the Kings will, but all is Subjected to his Authority: by which means it follows that he can do no wrong, nor can he receive wrong; and a King of England, keeping to these measures, may without arrogance be said to remain the onely Intelligent Ruler over a Rational people. In recompense therefore and acknowledgment of so good a Government under his Influence, his Person is most Sacred and Inviolable; and whatsoever Excesses are committed against so High a Trust, nothing of them is imputed to him, as being free from the Necessity or Temptation, but his Ministers only are Accountable for all, and must answer it [at?] their perils. He hath a vast Revenue constantly arising from the Hearth of the Householder, the Sweat of the Labourers, the Rent of the Farmer, the Industry of the Merchant, and consequently out of the Estate of the Gentleman a large competence to defray the ordinary expense of the

Crown, and maintain its lustre. And if any extraordinary Occasion happen, or be but with any probable decency pretended, the whole Land at whatsoever Season of the Year does yield him a plentiful Harvest. So forward are his Peoples Affections to give, even to superfluity, that a Forainer (or *English-man* that hath been long abroad) would think they could neither will nor chuse, but that the asking of a Supply, were a meer formality, it is so readily granted. He is the Fountain of all Honours, and has moreover the distribution of so many profitable Offices, of the Houshold, of the Revenue, of State, of Law, of Religion, of the Navy (and, since his present *Majesties* time, of the Army) that it seems as if the Nation could scarce furnish honest Men enow to supply all those Imployments. So that the Kings of *England* are in nothing Inferiour to other Princes, save in being more abridged from Injuring their own Subjects: But have as large a Field as any of external Felicity, wherein to exercise their own Vertue, and so reward and incourage it in others. In short, there is nothing that comes nearer in Government to the Divine perfection, than where the Monarch, as with us, enjoys a capacity of doing all the good imaginable to mankind, under a disability to all that is evil.

Andrew Marvell, *An Account Of the Growth of Popery, And Arbitrary Government in England* (1678), pp. 3–4

In offering this idealistic description of the English constitution Marvell makes his contribution to the debate on the nature of monarchy which had been going on since Shakespeare's day. Despite the efforts of supporters of the theory of the Divine Right of Kings, the idea that on their accession princes agreed to govern according to the law of the land became increasingly widespread as the seventeenth century progressed, and particularly after 1640. Behind the concept was the fear that, unchecked, royal authority might itself threaten the very things government was supposed to have been instituted in order to protect – the liberty and property of the individual. Adherents of this rival theory argued that, since political power ultimately derived from the people, monarchy in its pristine form was limited, or 'mixed', with the prince's power circumscribed by laws which prevented him from endangering the lives and liberties of his subjects. This, according to Marvell, was nearest 'in Government to the Divine perfection'. In contrast, continental monarchies, by moving towards absolutism, had usurped that power which had previously subsisted in the people.

Marvell referred to 'the Divine perfection' of the English monarchy because, as we have seen, his pamphlet was written in implicit contradiction of a very different ideological position. And although *An Account of the Growth of Popery* received its fair share of attention from the King's supporters, Sir Roger L'Estrange offering *An Account of the Growth of Knavery*, the debate quickly shifted its ground when the published works of Sir Robert Filmer were rushed into print once more in 1679 in a collected edition which included *The Anarchy of a Limited or Mixed Monarchy* (1648) and *Observations upon Aristotle's Politiques* (1652). Filmer was the patriarchalist *par excellence*. '*Adam* was the father, King and Lord over his family: a son, a subject, and a servant, or a slave, were one and the same thing at first', he argued. '[T]he father had power to dispose, or sell his children or servants, whence we finde, that at the first reckoning up of goods in Scripture, the man servant, and the maid servant are numbered among the possessions and substance of the owner as other goods were' (Filmer, *Observations*, Preface).

Although it would scarcely be possible to find a clearer equation of royal and patriarchal power, Filmer's major statement of political theory only appeared in January 1680, some years after it was written. In it he managed to take the panoply of Divine Right doctrines to their logical, if extreme, conclusion:

> SInce the time that School-Divinity began to flourish, there hath been a common Opinion maintained, as well by Divines, as by divers other learned Men, which affirms,
>
> *Mankind is naturally endowed and born with Freedom from all Subjection, and at liberty to choose what Form of Government it please: And that the Power which any one Man hath over others, were at first bestowed according to the discretion of the Multitude.*
>
> This Tenent was first hatched in the Schools, and hath been fostered by all succeeding Papists for good Divinity.

The Divines also of the Reformed Churches have entertained it, and the Common People every where tenderly embrace it, as being most plausible to Flesh and Blood, for that it prodigally destributes a Portion of Liberty to the meanest of the Multitude, who magnifie Liberty, as if the height of Humane Felicity were only to be found in it, never remembring That the desire of Liberty was the first Cause of the Fall of *Adam*.

But howsoever this Vulgar Opinion hath of late obtained a good Reputation, yet it is not to be found in the Ancient Fathers and Doctors of the Primitive Church: It contradicts the Doctrine and History of the Holy Scriptures, the constant Practice of all Ancient Monarchs, and the very Principles of the Law of Nature. It is hard to say whether it be more erroneous in Divinity, or dangerous in Policy.

Yet upon the ground of this Doctrine both *Jesuites*, and some other zealous favourers of the *Geneva* Discipline, have built a perillous Conclusion, which is, *That the People or* Multitude have Power to punish, or deprive the Prince, if he *transgress the Laws of the Kingdom* [. . .] This desperate Assertion whereby Kings are made subject to the *Censures* and *Deprivations of their Subjects*, follows (as the Authors of it conceive) as a necessary Consequence of that former Position of the supposed *Natural Equality and Freedom of Mankind, and Liberty to choose what form of Government it please* [. . .] The Rebellious Consequence which follows this prime Article of the *Natural Freedom of Mankind* may be my Sufficient Warrant for a modest Examination of the original Truth of it; much hath been said, and by many, for the *Affirmative*; Equity requires that an Ear be reserved a little for the *Negative* [. . .] To Answer this Reason, drawn from the Equality of Mankind by Nature, I will first use the help of *Bellarmine*[2] himself, whose very words are these: *If many men had been together created out of the Earth, they all ought to have been Princes over their Posterity*. In these words we have an Evident Confession, that Creation made man Prince of his Posterity. And indeed not only *Adam*, but the succeeding *Patriarchs* had, by Right of Father-hood, Royal Authority over their Children. Nor does *Bellarmine* deny this also. That the *Patriarchs* (saith he) were endowed with Kingly Power, their Deeds do testifie; for as *Adam* was Lord of his Children, so his Children under him, had a Command and Power over their own Children; but still with subordination to the First Parent, who is Lord-Paramou[n]t over his Childrens Children to all Generations, as being the *Grand-Father* of his People [. . .] I see not then how the Children of *Adam*, or of any man else can be free from subjection to their *Parents*: And this subjection of Children being the Fountain of all *Regal Authority*, by the Ordination of God himself; It follows, that Civil Power not only in general is by Divine Institution, but even the Assignment of it specifically to the Eldest Parents, which quite takes away that New and Common distinction, which refers only Power Universal and Absolute to God; but Power Respective, in regard of the Special Form of Government, to the Choice of the People.

This Lordship which *Adam* by Command had over the whole World, and by Right descending from him the *Patriarchs* did enjoy, was as large and ample as the Absolutest Dominion of any *Monarch* which hath been since the Creation [. . .] Not only until the *Flood*, but after it, this *Patriarchal Power* did continue, as the very name *Patriarch* doth in part prove [. . .] It may seem absurd to maintain that Kings now are the Fathers of the People, since Experience shews the contrary. It is true, all Kings be not the Natural Parents of their Subjects, yet they all either are, or are reputed the next Heirs to those first Progenitors, who were at first the Natural Parents of the whole People, and in their Right succeed to the Exercise of *Supreme Jurisdiction*; and such Heirs are not only Lords of their own Children, but also of their Brethren, and all others that were subject to their Fathers: And therefore we find, that God told *Cain* of his Brother *Abel*, *His Desires shall be subject unto thee, and thou shalt rule over him.* Accordingly, when *Jacob* bought his Brother's Birth-right, *Isaac* blessed him thus, *Be Lord over thy Brethren, and let the Sons of thy Mother bow before thee.*

As long as the first Fathers of Families lived, the name of *Patriarchs* did aptly belong unto them; but after a few

Descents, when the true Father-hood it self was extinct, and only the Right of the Father descends to the true Heir, then the Title of *Prince* or *King* was more *Significant*, to express the Power of him who succeeds only to the Right of that Fatherhood which his Ancestors did *Naturally* enjoy; by this means it comes to pass, that many a Child, by succeeding a King, hath the Right of a Father over many a Gray-headed Multitude, and hath the Title of *Pater Patriæ*.

Sir Robert Filmer, *Patriarcha: or the Natural Power of Kings*
(1680), pp. 2–5, 11–13, 19–20

Patriarcha generated a fierce controversy. It was answered both by James Tyrrell in *Patriarcha non Monarcha* (1680) and by Algernon Sidney in his *Discourses Concerning Government* (posthumously published in 1698), but the most famous refuter of Filmer's patriarchalist theories is John Locke. Peter Laslett has demonstrated that Locke's *Two Treatises of Government* was originally written as an Exclusionist tract. Indeed, as the title-page makes clear – 'In the Former [Treatise], The False Principles and Foundation of Sir Robert Filmer, And His Followers, Are Detected and Overthrown' – Locke takes pains to answer not merely *Patriarcha*, but Filmer's entire *æuvre*. As the following passage indicates, Locke is unable to leave Filmer alone even in his second treatise, as he sums up the fundamental difference between Filmer's patriarchal thinking and his own:

22. THE natural Liberty of Man is to be free from any Superiour Power on Earth, and not to be under the Will or Legislative Authority of Man, but to have only the Law of Nature for his Rule. The Liberty of Man, in Society, is to be under no other Legislative Power, that established, by consent, in the Commonwealth, nor under the Dominion of any Will, or Restraint of any Law, but what that Legislative shall enact, according to the Trust put in it. Freedom then is not what S[i]r R[obert]. F[ilmer]. tells us, *O[bservations upon] A[ristotle's Politiques,* p.] 55. *A Liberty for every one to do what he lists, to live as he pleases, and not to be tyed by any Laws*: but Freedom of Men, under Government, is, to have a standing Rule

to live by, common to every one of that Society, and made by the Legislative Power erected in it. A Liberty to follow my own Will in all things, where that Rule prescribes not; not to be subject to the inconstant, uncertain, unknown, Arbitrary Will of another Man. As Freedom of Nature is to be under no other restraint but the Law of Nature.

23. This Freedom from Absolute, Arbitrary Power, is so necessary to, and closely joyned with a Man's Preservation, that he cannot part with it, but by what forfeits his Preservation and Life together. For a Man, not having the Power of his own Life, cannot, by Compact, or his own Consent, enslave himself to any one, nor put himself under the Absolute, Arbitrary Power of another, to take away his Life, when he pleases. No body can give more Power than he has himself; and he that cannot take away his own Life, cannot give another Power over it.

John Locke, *Two Treatises of Government* (1690), pp. 241–2

In this way Locke sought to refute Filmer's sweeping insistence that fathers were originally able to dispose of their children in the same way that they might sell their servants or slaves. An important abstract principle is being espoused here – one which is so ingrained in modern thinking that it is perhaps difficult to conceive of a world which thought otherwise. 'T[o] understand Political Power a right, and derive it from its Original', Locke insisted, 'we must consider what Estate all Men are naturally in, and that is, a State of perfect Freedom to order their Actions, and dispose of their Possessions, and Persons as they think fit, within the bounds of the Law of Nature, without asking leave, or depending upon the Will of any other Man' (*Two Treatises*, p. 220). While Filmer and his Tory followers, working from their assumptions about Divine Right, denied man's natural freedom, Locke, showing how they confused liberty with licence, asserted the basic liberty and equality of all men.

People mostly agreed on the need for government and its purpose. It was necessary to wait until after the Revolution of 1688 and the actual publication of Locke's *Two Treatises* for an alternative view of the rise of society and a theory based on property, and we shall examine these in the next chapter. For the moment, let us concentrate on some of the ramifications of patriarchalist thought. Throughout the seventeenth century, as the rival political theories developed, supporters of Divine Right had pushed the idea that the monarch was *pater patriæ* – a father to his people – who would naturally have the interest and happiness of his subjects at heart. But if the prince were to be perceived as a bad king, then the paternalistic ideal tended to fall down. The Court of Charles II was notorious for its moral laxity and the King was habitually criticised for failing to provide a strong moral lead. The infamous lampoon for which Rochester was banished the Court (or so the story goes) exemplifies a Restoration literary tradition:

> IN the Isle of *Great Britain*, long since famous known,
> For breeding the Best [cunts] in *Christendom*;
> There Reigns, and long may he Reign and thrive,
> The easiest Prince, and best bred *Man* alive;
> Him no Ambition moves to seek Renown,
> Like the *French* Fool to wander up and down,
> Starving his Subjects, hazarding his Crown.
> [Peace is his aim, his gentleness is such,
> And love he loves, for he loves fucking much.]
> Nor are his high Desires above his Strength,
> His Scepter and his [prick] are of a length;
> And she that plays with one may sway the other
> And make him little wiser than his Brother.
> I hate all Monarchs, and the Thrones they sit on
> From the Hector of *France*, to the Cully of *Britain*.
> Poor Prince, thy [prick] like the Buffoons at Court,
> It governs thee, because it makes the Sport:
> ['Tis sure the sauciest prick that did ever swive,
> The proudest peremptoriest prick alive.]
> Tho' Safety, Law, Religion, Life lay on't,
> 'Twill break through all to make its way to [cunt.]
>   Restless he rolls about from Whore to Whore,
> A merry Monarch, scandalous and poor.
> To *Carewell* the most Dear of all his Dears,
> The sure Relief of his declining Years;
> Oft he bewails his Fortune and her Fate,
> To Love so well, and to be Lov'd so late.

For when in her, he settles well his [tarse,]
Yet his dull graceless Buttocks hang an Arse.
This you'd believe, had I but time to tell ye
The Pain it costs to poor laborious *Nelly*,
While she employs, Hands, Fingers, Lips and Thighs,
E'er she, can raise the *Member* she enjoys.

> John Wilmot, Earl of Rochester, *Miscellaneous
> Works* (1707), pp. 116–17

Here we see morals, manners, politics and literature intersecting.
Indeed, to speak of morals *and* manners in this period would
have been deemed more or less tautological. It was a political
matter. 'Tho' Safety, Law, Religion, Life lay on't', the King
seemed to be interested only in his own sexual satisfaction.
Rochester was not alone in making such an equation. 'His
Brother, his Minister and his Mistress play the game into one
another's hands', wrote Shaftesbury in criticism of Charles'
conduct, 'and perfectly govern all matters' (quoted in Jones, *The
First Whigs*, p. 59).

Rochester's satire was not untypical of its age: it was simply
the most outspoken attack of its kind. In another (anonymous)
poem, as Charles awaits the arrival of yet another sexual partner,
he is upbraided for his outrageous behaviour by the ghost of Sir
Edmund Berry Godfrey:

A Court you have with Luxury o'er-grown,
And all the Vices e'er in nature known;
Where Pimps and Pandors on their Coaches ride,
And in Lampoons and Songs your Lust deride.
Old Bawds and slighted Whores, there tell with shame,
The dulle Romance of your Lascivious Flame.

A New Collection of Poems Relating to State Affairs (1705), p. 87

As long as the sermon lasts, Charles seems repentant, but no
sooner has the harangue finished than his attention turns to
other matters:

The Ghost spake thus, groan'd thrice, and said no more;
Straight in came *Chiffinch*,[3] *hand* in *hand* with Whore;

The King, tho' much concern'd 'twixt Joy and Fear,
Starts from the Couch, and bids the Dame draw near.

A New Collection of Poems Relating to State Affairs (1705), p. 87

Even Dryden tacitly accepted criticism of Charles' inadequacies as head of state. *Absalom and Achitophel* opens with what amounts to implicit condemnation of the King's moral laxity, and towards the end of the poem Dryden once again draws attention to his manifold weaknesses. What is of greatest interest, however, is the way in which Dryden makes use of the idea of David as *pater patriæ*, and how he adapts it to defend Charles' policies so that what might otherwise be seen as poor leadership is transmogrified into a father's love for his people:

> With all these loads of Injuries opprest,
> And long revolving, in his carefull Breast,
> Th' event of things; at last his patience tir'd,
> Thus from his Royal Throne by heav'n inspir'd,
> The God-like *David* spoke: with awfull fear
> His Train their maker in their Master hear.
>   Thus long have I, by native mercy sway'd,
> My wrongs dissembl'd, my revenge delay'd:
> So willing to forgive th' Offending Age,
> So much the Father did the King asswage.
> But now so far my Clemency they slight,
> Th' Offenders question my Forgiving Right.
> That one was made for many, they contend:
> But 'tis to Rule, for that's a Monarch's End.
> They call my tenderness of Blood, my Fear:
> Though Manly tempers can the longest bear.
> Yet, since they will divert my Native course,
> 'Tis time to shew I am not Good by Force.
> Those heap'd Affronts that haughty Subjects bring,
> Are burthens for a Camel, not a King:
> Kings are the publick Pillars of the State,
> Born to sustain and prop the Nations weight [. . . .]

John Dryden, *Absalom and Achitophel* (1681), pp. 29–30

Absalom and Achitophel was published in November 1681, when the outcome of the Exclusion Crisis was no longer in any doubt. At the end of the same month Shaftesbury was due to stand trial on charges of treason – which is doubtless why Dryden's partisan and hopelessly prejudiced poem appeared when it did. Despite Dryden's worst efforts, however, Shaftesbury was acquitted by an equally partisan Whig jury. He wisely fled to Holland to die in exile early in 1683, by which time the King's party was rampant. Two other Whig leaders, Lord Russell and Algernon Sidney, were executed in the course of the same year for their alleged parts in the so-called Rye House Plot to assassinate the King on his way to the races at Newmarket, while a third, the Earl of Essex, committed suicide in the Tower. Evidence of a conspiracy involving these men is even more tenuous than that of the Popish Plot itself. They were simply victims of the authoritarian backlash which resulted from Charles II's victory over the Exclusionists. Having been drawn to the brink of another civil war, the political nation firmly decided in the short term in preference of the Tory doctrine of order, rather than risk the consequences of wholeheartedly embracing the various alternative ideologies propounded by Exclusionists of one kind or another.

The Tory reaction in the last years of the reign of Charles II was so extreme, in fact, that England seemed to be imitating other European monarchies in sliding towards absolutism. The concluding lines of *Absalom and Achitophel* vividly expressed the apparent triumph of Divine Right theory by insinuating that kings were indeed God's divinely-appointed lieutenants on earth, and therefore fathers of their people. Dryden immediately followed the speech of David (Charles II) with the following divine endorsement of Stuart policy:

> He said. Th' Almighty, nodding, gave Consent;
> And Peals of Thunder shook the Firmament.
> Henceforth a Series of new time began,
> The mighty Years in long Procession ran:
> Once more the Godlike *David* was Restor'd,
> And willing Nations knew their Lawfull Lord.

> John Dryden, *Absalom and Achitophel* (1681), p. 32

Charles II was peacefully succeeded on his death in 1685 by the man about whom all the fuss had been, his Roman Catholic brother, the former Duke of York, James II. The Parliament which met in May of that year was perhaps the most compliant to royal wishes of any in the entire course of the seventeenth century, and when in October 1685 the Duke of Monmouth, Dryden's Absalom, invaded England at the head of an army, the rebellion was quickly and easily put down by the King's loyal subjects. For the time being, Dryden's words appeared gloriously prophetic.

2 Revolution and Revolution Settlement

> If all our former Grievances were feign'd,
> King *James* has been abus'd, and we trepann'd;
> Bugbear'd with Popery and Power Despotick,
> Tyrannick Government, and Leagues Exotick:
> The Revolution's a Phanatick Plot,
> *W[illiam]* a Tyrant, *S[underland]*[4] a Sot:
> A Factious Army and a Poyson'd Nation,
> Unjustly forc'd King *James*'s Abdication.
> But if he did the Subjects Rights invade,
> Then he was punish'd only, not betray'd:
> *And punishing of Kings is no such Crime,*
> *But* Englishmen *ha' done it many a time.*
> When Kings the Sword of Justice first lay down,
> They are no Kings, though they possess the Crown.
>
> Daniel Defoe, *The True-Born Englishman:*
> *A Satyr* (1700), pp. 45–6

It took James II little more than three years to squander his subjects' good will. Embarking on a ruthless policy of Catholicisation which did nothing to damp down the fears expressed by the Exclusionists in the previous reign, the new King systematically alienated most sections of the political nation. A key element in this process was the expansion of the army after the suppression of the Monmouth Rebellion. Officered by Catholics in open defiance of the terms of the Test Act, the army was quartered in the provinces 'so that by 1688 the whole kingdom was taking on the appearance of a country under military occupation' (J. R. Jones (ed.), *The Restored Monarchy 1660–1688* (1979), p. 18).

Whereas during the Exclusion Crisis fears about arbitrary government and Popery had been expressed by only part of the privileged elite, in 1688 they were shared by virtually everyone. When Queen Mary gave birth to a son in June of that year, it was the final straw. Until then James's heir had been his Protestant daughter, Mary, the wife of William of Orange, Stadtholder of the Dutch United Provinces. Now the prospect was not merely one of a short reign by a Catholic King, but of a Catholic dynasty. William was encouraged to uphold the rights not only of his wife, but of the nation at large. On 5 November 1688 he landed with an army at Torbay in the west country. Posing as the defender of the rights and privileges of Englishmen, as the printed *Declaration of his Reasons for Appearing in Arms in the Kingdom of England* makes clear, William simply waited while support for James finally evaporated. The King fled, only to be prevented by Kentish fishermen from reaching France. As his presence in England was by this stage more of an embarrassment than anything else, James was permitted to escape a second time, setting foot on French soil on Christmas Day 1688.

Thus were established the prevailing conditions of British politics for the succeeding sixty years. In the short term James's flight settled nothing. The political nation could not just pretend that the reigning King no longer existed and pass on to another monarch. That would not resolve the massive constitutional problems occasioned by the events of 1688. For a start, the solution to the relatively straightforward question of the actual succession was far from obvious. Mary was James II's elder daughter by his first marriage, but it had been the birth of a son to his second wife which had brought affairs to a crisis in the first place. Even if a decision were made to pass over this new-born fruit of a Catholic marriage, and offer the Crown to Mary in an attempt to retain some semblance of hereditary succession, what about William of Orange, Mary's husband, who was presently in England at the head of an army? It was scarcely likely that, having taken the tremendous risk of crossing the English Channel with a comparatively small contingent of Dutchmen, he would simply acquiesce in an outcome which did not leave him in control of the nation's affairs. William needed England to play the role of a principal in the European alliance he was trying to produce in opposition to the aggressive foreign policy of the France of Louis XIV.

Some flavour of the constitutional debates which took place

during January and February 1689 can be derived from the proceedings of the Convention Parliament. On 28 January the House of Commons resolved

> That King *James* the Second, having endeavoured to subvert the Constitution of the Kingdom, by breaking the Original Contract between King and People; and, by the Advice of Jesuits, and other wicked Persons, having violated the fundamental Laws; and having with-drawn himself out of the Kingdom; has abdicated the Government and that the Throne is thereby vacant.
>
> *Journals of the House of Commons*, X, 14

This version of events laid the blame firmly at James's door, insinuating that his flight was an indication of his wish to abdicate. And if James had indeed abdicated, then it could be argued that the throne was vacant. But mention of 'the Original Contract between King and People' flew in the face of Divine Right theory and attempted to settle the debates over the nature of the monarchy which, as we saw in the previous chapter, had been going on since the reign of Elizabeth I.

Awareness of implications such as these was behind the amendments to the resolution proposed by the House of Lords. Not only was there the insistence that the word 'deserted' should replace 'abdicated', but their Lordships wished the final clause – 'and that the Throne is thereby vacant' – to be omitted. Their reasoning was made evident in a conference between the two Houses called when it became clear that they were unlikely to agree:

> Abdication is a voluntary express Act of Renunciation, which is not in this Case [. . .] the Lords were and are willing to secure the Nation against the Return of the said King into this Kingdom; but not that there was either such an abdication by him, or such a Vacancy in the Throne, as that the Crown was thereby become Elective.
>
> To which they cannot agree.
> I. Because, by the Constitution of the Government, the Monarchy is hereditary, and not elective.

> 2. Because no Act of the King alone can bar or destroy
> the Right of his Heirs to the Crown [. . . .]
>
> *Journals of the House of Commons*, X, 19–20

Contemporaries recognised that a great deal was at issue here.
The nature of the English monarchy was being debated early in
1689, not just the more straightforward question of who should
be king. And even bigger and more dangerous issues were
suspected with reason to be lurking further on down the road.
As John Toland put it only a few years later, it was probable that
most people 'never thought during one hour of the Original or
End of Societies, till the late Differences gave 'em an opportunity
and incouragement to do it' (*The Militia Reform'd* (1698), p. 9).

After 1689 this was true no longer and, as we shall see, the
literature of the period is shot through with allusions to such
matters. Over twenty years later, when he was trying to explain
how political parties had developed in England, Jonathan Swift
remarked on the importance of what had happened in January
and February 1689:

> In that Convention of Lords and Commons, some of
> both Houses were for a *Regency* to the Prince of *Orange*,
> with a Reservation of Style and Title to the absent King,
> which should be made use of in all Publick Acts.
> Others, when they were brought to allow the Throne
> vacant, thought the Succession should immediately go to
> the next Heir, according to the Fundamental Laws of the
> Kingdom, as if the last King were actually dead. And
> tho' the Dissenting Lords (in whose House the chief
> Opposition was) did at last yield both those Points, took
> the Oaths to the new King, and many of them Employ-
> ments, yet they were look'd upon with an evil Eye by the
> warm Zealots of the other side; neither did the Court
> ever heartily favour any of them, though some were of
> the most eminent for Abilities and Virtue, and serv'd
> that Prince, both in his Councils and his Army, with
> untainted Faith. It was apprehended, at the same time,
> and perhaps it might have been true, that many of the
> Clergy would have been better pleas'd with that Scheme
> of a *Regency*, or at least an uninterrupted lineal Succes-

sion, for the sake of those whose Conscences were truly *Scrupulous*; and they thought there were some Circumstances, in the Case of the depriv'd Bishops, that look'd a little hard, or at least deserv'd Commiseration.

These, and other the like Reflections did, as I conceive, revive the Denominations of *Whig* and *Tory*.

Jonathan Swift, *The Examiner* No. 44: 24–31 May 1711

The various effects of the Revolution Settlement to which Swift is referring will be considered in their place. In the immediate aftermath of 1688, the most pressing matter was one of securing the subject's allegiance. By no means everyone was as easily reconciled to the new regime as Swift, who was evidently influenced by the radical political ideas of John Locke. Many were unable, in all conscience, to submit to the new order or to take the oaths of allegiance and supremacy to William and Mary. These 'nonjurors', as they were called, automatically disqualified themselves from public office. To all intents and purposes they were in much the same circumstances as Roman Catholics – second-class citizens who were forced to sacrifice their civil rights as a consequence of their beliefs. Nonjuring clergymen were hit particularly hard, as their failure to take the oaths meant that they were deprived of their livings. William Sancroft, the Archbishop of Canterbury, was accompanied into the wilderness by five bishops and around 400 clergymen of other ranks.

Their difficulty was ideological as much as theological. How could men who had previously held on with some tenacity to the doctrines of indefeasible hereditary succession, passive obedience and non-resistance, simply swear allegiance to William and Mary as sovereigns while James II was living in exile in France? There were three main avenues open to those who thought in this way in 1689. One, as we have noted, was simply to refuse to take the oaths and to retire from public life in respect to the notion of passive obedience. While the nonjurors were also in some sense passive Jacobites, this label should more strictly be reserved for those who actively worked for the restoration of James II and his descendants. Early Jacobite publications emphasised the inadequacy of the political fictions of 'abdication' and 'vacancy' to justify the Revolution Settlement.

But there was a broader band of opinion: those who, although they were uncomfortable with the idea of taking the oaths of allegiance and supremacy to William and Mary, were looking for a convincing explanation which would satisfy their conscientious objections.

The last of these were the principal targets of government propaganda. The first ploy was an attempt to supply an 'official' version of events which, like Marvell's famous pamphlet, operated on the assumption that England had been the victim of a conspiracy 'to change the Lawful Government [...] into an Absolute Tyranny, and to Convert the Established Protestant Religion into down-right Popery'. This was the purpose of Edmund Bohun's *History of the Desertion*, dated 6 April 1689, as the sub-title – 'An Account of all the Publick Affairs in England, From the beginning of September 1688 to the Twelfth of February following' – makes abundantly clear. Bohun's preface tried to supervise the way in which his ostensibly objective account would be read:

> I conceive this short Abstract of the Publick Printed Papers, is sufficient to convince any Man, that the *Popish Party* were resolved we should be Rebels, (as they now account us) or Slaves; and His late Majesty was so far prevailed upon by them, that he chose rather to desert his *Throne*, than to lose all the Possibilities of Establishing an absolute Soveraignty over the Nation, and *Popery* with it.
>
> I suppose it is not pretended in *England*, His Late Majesty forfeited his Right to Govern by his Misgovernment; but that the sense of it prevail'd upon him rather to throw up the Government, than to concur with an *English* Free-Parliament in all that was needful to re-establish our *Laws*, *Liberties* and *Religion*; and this is a proper legal *Abdication*, as it is distinguished from a Voluntary *Resignation* on the one hand, and a Violent *Deposition* on the other.
>
> He was bound to govern us according to Law, and we were not bound to submit to any other than a legal Government; but he would not do the one, and saw he could not force us to submit to the other, and therefore deliberately relinquish'd the *Throne*, and withdrew his

Person and Seals, dissolving (as much as he could) the whole Frame of our Government.

Edmund Bohun, *The History of the Desertion* (1689), Preface

Bohun's narrative was quickly followed by *A Pastoral Letter Writ By The Right Reverend Father in God Gilbert, Lord Bishop of Sarum, To the Clergy of his Diocese, Concerning The Oaths of Allegiance and Supremacy to K[ing] William and Q[ueen] Mary*. Actually a sort of late-seventeenth-century 'open letter' from King William's propagandist, Gilbert Burnet, Bishop of Salisbury, this pamphlet sought to tell more than its putative addressees how to behave. Its 'official' character can be appreciated by the fact that not only was it licensed for publication on 16 May 1689, it carried the caption: 'Publish'd By Her Majesty's Command':

> which way soever that King *James*'s deserting the Government is turned, this Argument has much weight; for if he was forced to it, then here was a Conquest; and if it was voluntary, it was a wilful Desertion: the Great Seal's being cast into the *Thames*, is an unaccountable part of it, and seems to imply this at least, That either he did not think of returning again, or that if he should return, that he would no more Govern by the shew of Law, of which the Great Seal seems always to carry some Prints.
>
> So that, in a word, the People of *England* being left without a Government, and in the Hands of one that could and might have assumed it, and that stood so near the immediate Succession to the Crown, were reduced to the necessity, either of continuing in a State of Anarchy [. . .] or of returning to the Misery which they had so much dreaded but a few Months before, or of settling themselves upon such a legal Foundation as might secure the Peace and Quiet of the Nation [. . . .]

Gilbert Burnet, *A Pastoral Letter* (1689), pp. 21–3

The tone is as conciliatory as possible: because James's desertion was an established fact, the only matter of debate, according to Burnet, was whether he had been forced to it or whether he had done it voluntarily. If the former, then William was rightfully king by conquest; if the latter, then James had indeed abdicated, in which case it was right and proper for one 'that stood so near the immediate Succession of the Crown' to assume the government, and rescue the nation from the disastrous consequences of impending anarchy.

What proved to be an even more powerful argument was offered by the quondam Dean of St Paul's Cathedral, William Sherlock, who set out to prove the following propositions 'from the Authority of Scripture and Reason':

> If then Allegiance be due, not for the sake of Legal Right, but Government.
>
> If Allegiance be due, not to bare Legal Right, but to the Authority of God.
>
> If God, when he sees fit, and can better serve the ends of his Providence by it, sets up Kings without any regard to Legal Right, or Humane Laws.
>
> If Kings, thus set up by God, are invested with Gods Authority, which must be obeyed, not only for wrath, but also for conscience sake.
>
> If these Principles be true, it is plain, that Subjects are bound to obey, and to pay and swear Allegiance (if it be required) to those Princes whom God hath placed and settled in the Throne, whatever Disputes there may be about their legal Right, when they are invested with God's Authority.
>
> And then it is plain, that our old Allegiance and old Oaths are at an end, when God has set over us a new King: for when God transfers Kingdoms, and requires our Obedience and Allegiance to a new King, he necessarily transfers our Allegiance too.

> William Sherlock, *The Case of Allegiance due to Soveraign Powers, Stated and Resolved* (1691), pp. 2–3

What was original and clever about Sherlock's argument was the way it effectively turned the notion of passive obedience on its head: drawing on Romans 13, even *The Whole Duty of Man* had insisted that 'We owe such an *obedience* to the supreme power, that whoever is authorised by [God], we are to submit to' so that 'we are then bound to act according to that command of the Magistrate, to do the thing he requires' (p. 280). It was not for the obedient subject to try to fathom the mysterious workings of Divine Providence. His duty was merely to submit to the 'higher powers', for 'the powers that be are ordained of God'.

Sherlock's interpretation of scriptural injunctions on authority and allegiance convinced many Tory adherents of Divine Right doctrine that it was appropriate for them to take the oaths to William and Mary as sovereigns *de facto*, while continuing to recognise James II as King *de iure*. Their willingness to follow Sherlock's example was perhaps helped by the fact that the former Dean of St Paul's had at first been a nonjuror himself and had therefore been deprived of his living. Thus his own change of heart might be regarded as conscientious – the result of lengthy meditation on the theological problems posed by the Revolution. Not that that was how Sherlock's altered opinion was viewed by others. To the Jacobites and to those who remained nonjurors he was a turncoat who had capitulated to the new regime to serve his own ends. To the Whigs Sherlock was an equivocator who was not prepared to come out and acknowledge the legitimacy of the Revolution Settlement.

As far as the Whigs were concerned, the Revolution posed few problems in the short term and none whatsoever of a conscientious nature. They were firm supporters of 'Revolution Principles'. As a consequence they cared nothing for nice distinctions between sovereigns *de facto* and sovereigns *de iure*. James II had tried to undermine the constitution, therefore it was only right and proper that he had been replaced by another at the people's behest. Radical Whigs wanted nothing to do with any of the other explanations which had been put forward to justify the Revolution either, as Samuel Johnson's appropriately-titled pamphlet, *An Argument Proving, That the Abrogation of King James by the People of England from the Regal Throne, and the promotion of the Prince of Orange, one of the Royal Family, to the Throne of the Kingdom in his stead, was according to the Constitution of the English Government, and Prescribed by it. In Opposition to all the false and treacherous Hypotheses, of Usurpation, Conquest, Desertion, and of taking the Powers that Are upon Content*, makes absolutely clear:

> These wretched Inventions of *Usurpation, Conquest*, and *Desertion*, were found out meerely to cover the Doctrine

of Passive Obedience, and to keep that safe and sound, notwithstanding the Prince and the whole Nation had engag'd in Resisting Oppression; and Defending their Rights. And furthermore, That King *William*'s coming to the Crown might not be enquir'd into, and be found to be [to?] the Prejudice of Non-resistance, There is one has likewise found out another Invention, That you are not to trouble your Head, whether the King's Title be right or wrong, but you are to Swear to whatever is Uppermost, whether he be a Rightful Prince or an Usurper; which is the Primitive Doctrine of the Pastoral Letter.

And this is such a Scorn put upon a Free Nation as never was in the World, as if the Subjects of *England* were to engage their Allegiance Blindfold, and were to venture their Lives and Fortunes in behalf of a Title which is to be unsight unseen, at that ridiculous rate as no Country-man will buy a Pig.

Now all these Hypotheses have but these two small Faults in common to them all.

First, That they Undermine the King's Throne, as if he had no Legal Right to the Crown; And if he has not, what has he to do with it? For my part I will never pay Allegiance to him as an Usurper; he ought rather to be told daily by his Chaplains that are of that mind, that he ought to make Restitution: *It is not Lawful for thee to have thy Father James['s] Crown*; or else they are no St. *John Baptists*. A Revelation sent on purpose from Heaven, cannot oblige us to be Subjects to an Usurper under that Notion, because it is a Notion of Wrong, and God himself cannot make Wrong to be Right. And then shall any Wretch bid us in his Name to Swear to be Faithful to acknowledged Wrong, and to be False to acknowledged and unextinguished Right? In short, an Usurped Crown is a Stol'n Crown, it is *Blood*'s Crown.

It is true that God can give Kingdoms to whomsoever he will; I know it; He can make them a New World on purpose for them, or take the Forfeiture of the Old, and dispose of his own Creation as he pleases: But then it must appear to [be?] his Will, and he must send a New Revelation into the World along with such a highly

Favoured Prince, to every Man that is to be his Subject. For I am not bound to do what God would have me do, till I can certainly know that he would have me do it. Promulgation is of the Essence of a Law.

And this Extraordinary Revelation ought to be as clear and as distinct as *Abraham*'s was for the Sacrificing his Son; for it is as contrary to all the settled Rules of Right to dethrone a Rightful King as it is to destroy an only Son.

Samuel Johnson, *An Argument Proving, That the Abrogation of King James by the People of England* (1692), pp. 9–10

Perhaps because he, too, was a clergyman, Johnson's discourse is recognisably that of Allestree, Burnet and Sherlock. Despite his political ideology he was concerned to try to reconcile the theoretical foundations of the English constitution with the authority of Scripture, for it was the Christian religion which underpinned the social structure. The discourse of John Locke, however, was of another kind. Although, as we have seen, the first of his *Two Treatises of Government* was given over to refuting 'the False Principles, and Foundation of Sir Robert Filmer, and His Followers' – a clear indication of the longevity of patriarchalist thought as well as the doctrines of passive obedience and non-resistance – Locke's book was avowedly published 'to establish the Throne of our great Restorer, Our present King *William*, [and] to make good his Title, in the Consent of the People' (Preface). To this end the second treatise, 'An Essay concerning the True Original, Extent, and End of Civil Government', introduced a different way of looking at the world.

Like Hobbes before him, Locke first envisaged mankind in a state of nature, before the restraints on human behaviour required by society had been put in place. In this state of 'equality of Men by Nature', every man was free to do whatever he wished, and 'to have only the Law of Nature for his Rule'. As there was no society as yet, there could of course be no civil laws, and therefore nò magistrate or 'Superiour Power' to ensure that these were carried out. But there were disadvantages to being in such a state of nature. 'The great and chief end [. . .] of Mens uniting into Commonwealths, and putting themselves under Government, is the preservation of their Property', Locke explained. 'To which in the state of Nature there are many things wanting' (p. 346). Men therefore contracted to enter into society by agreeing to live according to laws enacted with their consent. These laws were executed by a sovereign power which, in the case of England, was a monarch.

Although Locke's thesis that society was formed by a social contract and government by a fiduciary trust was radical enough, presenting an even greater challenge to Divine Right theory than the concept of limited monarchy propounded by Marvell, its ramifications extended still further. *Two Treatises of Government* sought to justify the succession of William III by insisting that, ultimately, political power always subsisted in the people and that the role of the monarch was simply an executive one. If therefore the monarch forfeited the trust which had been placed in him (which was clearly the case as far as James II was concerned), then the executive power 'reverts to the Society, and the People have a Right to act as Supreme, and continue the Legislative in themselves, or place it in a new Form, or new hands, as they think good' (p. 271). Locke implied that in 1689 the Convention Parliament, the representative body of the people, had plumped for the most conservative option, retaining the institution of monarchy but placing the Crown in different hands. If this were true, then Locke had achieved his aim of making good William's title as King by consent of the people.

The Convention Parliament had decided to keep faith with the notion of a 'mixed monarchy', but it would have been equally consistent with Locke's thesis to have done away with the monarchy altogether, and to have set up a republic in its stead. Because of the indisputably radical nature of his discourse, there is a danger that the massively conservative underpinning of Locke's ideas can be forgotten. The underlying purpose of *Two Treatises* was the theoretical justification of the rights and privileges of the propertied elite. Locke might have insisted on the 'equality of Men by Nature', but he was no leveller. Instead, he was a staunch advocate of the hierarchical structure of society. To appreciate this to the full it is perhaps necessary to look in more detail at what he says about property:

> 27. Though the Earth, and all inferior Creatures be common to all Men, yet every Man has a *Property* in his own *Person*. This no Body has any Right to but himself.

The *Labour* of his Body, and the *Work* of his Hands, we may say, are properly his. Whatsoever then he removes out of the State that Nature hath provided, and left it in, he hath mixed his Labour with it, and joined to it something that is his own, and thereby makes it his Property. It being by him removed from the common state Nature placed it in, it hath by this labour something annexed to it, that excludes the common right of other Men. For this *labour* being the unquestionable Property of the Labourer, no Man but he can have a right to what that is once joined to, at least where there is enough, and as good left in common for others.

28. He that is nourished by the Acorns he pickt up under an Oak, or the Apples he gathered from the Trees in the Wood; has certainly appropriated them to himself. No Body can deny but the nourishment is his. I ask then, when did they begin to be his? When he digested? or when he eat? Or when he boiled? Or when he brought them home? Or when he pickt them up? And 'tis plain, if the first gathering made them not his, nothing else could. That labour put a distinction between them and common. That added something to them more than Nature, the common Mother of all, had done; and so they became his private right. And will any one say he had no right to those Acorns or Apples he thus appropriated, because he had not the consent of all Mankind to make them his? Was it a Robbery thus to assume to himself what belonged to all in Common? If such a consent as that was necessary, Man had starved, notwithstanding the Plenty God had given him. We see in Commons, which remain so by Compact, that 'tis the taking any part of what is common, and removing it out of the state Nature leaves it in, which begins the Property; without which the Common is of no use. And the taking of this or that part, does not depend on the express consent of all the Commoners. Thus the Grass my Horse has bit; the Turfs my Servant has cut; and the Ore I have dig'd in any place where I have a right to them in common with others, become my Property, without the assignation or consent of any body. The labour that was mine, removing them out of

that common state they were in, hath fixed my Property
in them.

John Locke, *Two Treatises of Government* (1690), pp. 245–7

On first reading, Locke's views on property might seem liberal
enough. After all, he generously allows every man a basic
property in his own person and the right to enjoy the fruits of
his own labour. And he does take pains, through a series of
rhetorical questions, to establish the precise point at which
property begins. But there are certain ideological silences in
Locke's text which might be interrogated in a similar way. If
labour is 'the unquestionable Property of the Labourer', as Locke
asserts, then why do the turfs cut by his servant become Locke's
property and not the property of the actual labourer? How does
the servant's labour become Locke's? Where, in fact, has the
servant come from? Locke's discourse seems to omit an entire
stage of social development from a state of nature in which all
men are free and equal to a society in which only certain men
(and not women of course) are permitted to acquire property.
   Although, because of its radical character, the theoretical
justification of the existence of a propertied elite offered in *Two
Treatises* created less of a stir in the years immediately following
the Revolution than Sherlock's *The Case of Allegiance due to
Soveraign Powers*, Locke's views gradually gained currency at the
expense of the rival theory of the Divine Right of Kings. This
was largely because he had isolated the two main props of the
existing social order. First, there was the gamut of rights and
privileges that constituted the liberty of the individual and which
needed to be safeguarded against the encroachments of arbitrary
monarchy. Secondly, there was property, particularly real estate,
the possession of which was the distinguishing factor between
the privileged elite and the rest of mankind. Liberty and property
were the watchwords of the 1690s, in direct opposition to the
patriarchalist views which had held the field for most of the
previous decade. When Robert Molesworth wrote *An Account of
Denmark, As It was in the Year 1692*, he chose to begin in this
way:

H*Ealth* and *Liberty* are without dispute the greatest
natural Blessings Mankind is capable of enjoying; I say

natural, because the contrary states are purely accidental, and arise from Nature debauched, depraved or enforced. Yet these Blessings are seldom sufficiently valued whilst enjoy'd; like the daily advantages of the Sun and Air, they seem scarce regarded because so common, by those that are in possession of them.

But as an *Italian* who passes a Winter in *Groenland* [*sic*], will soon be convinc'd through his want of the kind Influences of that glorious Planet, how much Misery he endures, in comparison of those who dwell in his Native Country, so he that knows by Experience the trouble of a languishing Sickness, or the loss of his *Liberty*, will presently begin to have a right esteem of that which formerly he scarce thought worth his notice [...] Want of *Liberty* is a Disease in any Society or Body Politick, like want of *Health* in a particular Person; and as the best way to understand the nature of any Distemper aright, is to consider it in several Patients, since the same Disease may proceed from different causes, so the disorders in Society are best perceived by observing the Nature and Effects of them in our several Neighbours [...] He that travels into a Climate infected with this Disease (and he can find few that are not) does not only see, but in some measure feel the Grievances occasioned by it in the several Inconveniencies of living, in some proportion with the Natives; so as to relish better upon his return (which we suppose depends upon his choice) the freedom and ease of his home Constitution; and may make good use of this Experience without having paid too dear for it: But a man cannot transmigrate himself for a while into a distemper'd Body as he may travel into an enslaved Country, with equal facility of getting rid of each of them again.

Robert Molesworth, *An Account of Denmark* (1694), Preface

Molesworth's real subject was of course the state of England, not Denmark, and his was no mere traveller's tale. Years later in *Gulliver's Travels* Swift used a similar device when he described the laws and customs of the Lilliputians, Brobdingnagians and Houyhnhnms respectively. Underlying Molesworth's paean to

English liberty was the fear of a return to arbitrary government despite the events of 1688. That was why he decided to chronicle Denmark's slide into absolutism and what he chose to call slavery. The purpose was to inculcate one way of looking at the world in the reader rather than another, and *An Account of Denmark* was seminal in its description of the corruption of a nation's manners.

The political ideas propounded by Molesworth were usually subsumed into a wider tradition known as 'Country' ideology. It has already been remarked that in this period manners and morals were more or less tautological. Manners were the social customs of a people, the unspoken assumptions upon which their society was based. Implicit in Molesworth's account is the celebration of England's hierarchical social structure and condemnation of any deviation from this ideal. Country ideology often maintained that the nation's liberties were founded on an 'ancient constitution' which had its origins in Anglo-Saxon times. This 'Gothic' constitution was preserved by a careful balance of the three estates, King, Lords and Commons. If one of the three components were allowed to predominate, then the result would be the corruption of the body politic into either tyranny, oligarchy or anarchy. Therefore it was crucial for landowners to provide moral as well as economic leadership, as the healthiness of the constitution could be ensured only by those who were economically independent. Freemen could not be bought off by an encroaching executive. They alone could maintain civic virtue and preserve the manners of the people which, in turn, were essential to the continuation of the existing social order.

Therefore Chapter VIII of Molesworth's *Account of Denmark*, which told of 'The Condition, Customs, and Temper of the People', was central to his thesis:

> ALL these do so necessarily depend upon, and are influenced by the Nature and Change of Government, that 'tis easily imagined, the present Condition of these People of all Ranks must be most deplorable; at least it appears so to an *English* man, who sees it, possibly more than to them that suffer it: for Slavery, like a sickly Constitution, grows in time so habitual, that it seems no Burden nor Disease; it creates a kind of laziness, and idle despondency, which puts Men beyond hopes and fears:

it mortifies Ambition, Emulation, and other trouble-
some, as well as active qualities, which Liberty and
Freedom beget; and instead of them affords only a dull
kind of Pleasure of being careless and insensible. In
former Times, and even till the late Alteration in Government, the Nobility and Gentry (for they are here the
same thing) lived in great Affluence and Prosperity; their
Country Seats were large and magnificent, their Hospit-
ality extraordinary, because their Plenty was so too; they
lived for the most part at home, and spent their
Revenues among their Neighbours and Tenants, by
whom they were considered, and respected as so many
petty Princes. In times of Convention of the Estates,
which ordinarily happened once a year, they met with
their King with Retinues almost as large as his; they
frequently eat, and drank at the same Table with him,
and in the debate of Publick Affairs, their Suffrages were
of greatest weight, and usually carried the Point: for the
Commons were willing in a great measure to be directed
by them, because they much depended on them. In
process of time this Excess of Power, as you have heard,
made most of them grow insolent, which was the chief
occasion of their fall, together with the loss of the
Liberties of the whole Country. So that now they are
sunk to a very low Condition, and diminish daily both in
Number and Credit; their Estates scarce paying the
Taxes imposed on them: which makes them grind the
Faces of their poor Tenants to get an Overplus for their
own Subsistance.

Robert Molesworth, *An Account of Denmark* (1694), pp. 75–6

A dissipated gentry could hardly be expected to fulfil its traditional duties. If Divine Right theory insisted that kings were
fathers of their people, Country ideology stressed a different sort
of paternalism. Landlords were supposed to care for their
dependants, both materially and morally, therefore the condition
of their tenants was of the first importance. Neglect of the
landlord's paternalistic role would only lead to trouble. Not only
was it morally wrong, it threatened the stability of the social
system. If the people were to be kept in order, then the system

had not merely to work, it had to be seen to be working, so that the social reality – the possession by a few individuals of most of the power and wealth – would not be questioned.

This, of course, is why writers like Swift spent so much time criticising the conduct of landlords. It was fundamental to the hierarchical concept of society shared by almost all of the propertied elite that political power should be located only in the hands of men like themselves. Thus the distinction between freeman and servant was crucial to Country ideology, and for this it was indebted to the political philosophy of James Harrington. The first order of Harrington's 'Modell of The Common-Wealth of Oceana' divided '**the people into Freemen or Citizens, and Servants**', because, he explained, '**if they attain unto *Liberty*, that is, to live of themselves, they are *Freemen* or *Citizens*'.**[5] 'This Order needeth no proof, in regard of the nature of servitude', Harrington argued, which is inconsistent with Freedom or Participation of *Government* in a *Common-wealth*' (James Harrington, *The Common-Wealth of Oceana* (1656), p. 58). John Toland agreed. As his 'First Proposition' for increasing the effectiveness of the militia he put the following:

> That *ENGLAND* consisting of Freemen and Servants, none be capable of serving in the Militia but the former. By Freemen I understand Men of Property, or Persons that are able to live of themselves; and those who cannot subsist in this Independence, I call Servants. The bare Explication of the Terms should, one would think, be sufficient to perswade any Man of Sense that the former should not only be sooner trusted with Arms than the latter; but that they must needs use 'em likewise to better purpose. For besides that all the Endowments which Nature has made common to both are improv'd in Freemen, the very Temper of their Bodies being much stronger and livelier by better feeding, which is no little Ingredient to Courage, they fight also for their Liberty and Property; whereas the other have nothing to lose but their Lives, which are likewise infinitely dearer to those whose Circumstances render 'em more agreeable and easy.

John Toland, *The Militia Reform'd* (1698), pp. 18–19

We can glimpse the hidden agenda behind the ruling elite's preoccupation with manners in Toland's callous explanation of why the militia should exclude those who had no other property to lose than their lives. Massively conservative, resisting any change which would threaten his position in society, the landed man sought to perpetuate his traditional place in the social hierarchy under the banner of liberty and property.

He was fighting a battle he was doomed to lose. Toland was contributing to the controversy over a standing army which erupted on the conclusion of the Nine Years War in 1697 with the Treaty of Ryswick. Although a clear-cut victory had been won by neither side, hostilities petering out in a sort of stalemate, William III had achieved his main aim of countering the aggressive foreign policy of France. In addition, the end of the war meant that, in the short term at least, the English succession was secure as Louis XIV had recognised William as *de facto* King of England.

However, the domestic consequences of fighting an expensive war were immense. Although it took contemporaries many years to recognise, and still more to accept the fact, the war had changed everything. In order to finance it, the revenue of taxation had been anticipated through the raising of huge loans, secured by the foundation of the Bank of England in 1694. The Bank also regulated the interest paid on these loans, and arrangements were made for this to be covered by current taxation. The resulting financial revolution not only threatened the traditional position in society of the landed interest, it actually appeared to shift the balance of economic power to those with property, not in real estate, but in stocks and shares. Swift traced the development in his first *Examiner* paper:

> It was argued, that the War could not last above two or three Campaigns, and that it was easier for the Subject to raise a Fund for paying Interest, than to tax them annually to the full Expence of the War. Several Persons who had small or encumber'd Estates, sold them, and turn'd their Money into those Funds to great Advantage: Merchants, as well as other moneyed Men, finding Trade was dangerous, pursued the same Method: But the War continuing, and growing more expensive, Taxes were encreased, and Funds multiplied every Year, till they

have arrived at the monstrous height we now behold them. And that which was at first a Corruption, is at last grown necessary, and what every good Subject must fall in with, tho' he may be allowed to wish it might soon have an End; because it is with a Kingdom, as with a private Fortune, where every new Incumbrance adds a double weight. By this means the Wealth of the Nation, that used to be reckoned by the Value of Land, is now computed by the Rise and Fall of Stocks: And altho' the Foundation of Credit be still the same, and upon a Bottom that can never be shaken; and though all Interest be duly paid by the Publick, yet through the Contrivance and Cunning of *Stock-jobbers*, there has been brought in such a Complication of Knavery and Couzenage, such a Mystery of Iniquity, and such an unintelligible Jargon of Terms to involve it in, as were never known in any other Age or Country of the World.

Jonathan Swift, *The Examiner* No. 14: 2 November 1710

   Augustan satire is based to a large extent on a reaction to such developments. Satire is predominantly a conservative mode which habitually works by contrasting what is with what should be, and therefore satirists by their very nature are often critical of deviations from tradition. It is no coincidence that the great age of English satire followed on closely from a period of acute political instability or that the greatest satirists persistently be-moaned the passing of the old ways and the introduction of the new. Like most conservatives they hated and feared social change. 'We have seen a great part of the Nation's Mony got into the Hands of those, who by their Birth, Education and Merit', Swift insisted, 'could pretend no higher than to wear our Liveries' (*The Examiner* No. 15: 9 November 1710). Pope's famous ironic apostrophe to the newly-instituted system of public credit drew attention to another unfortunate by-product of this brave new world:

> Blest paper-credit! last and best supply!
> That lends Corruption lighter wings to fly!
> Gold imp'd by thee, can compass hardest things,
> Can pocket States, can fetch or carry Kings;

A single leaf shall waft an Army o'er,
Or ship off Senates to a distant Shore:
A leaf, like Sibyl's, scatter to and fro
Our fates and fortunes, as the winds shall blow:
Pregnant with thousands flits the Scrap unseen,
And silent sells a King, or buys a Queen.

Alexander Pope, *Epistles to Several Persons* (1743), pp. 45–6

It would not be stretching the point to suggest that far-reaching developments such as these were direct consequences of the Revolution and the Revolution Settlement. By 1697, and the standing army controversy, contemporaries were already questioning the extent of the social changes which were being brought about. What was actually happening in these years was the gradual working out of the practical consequences of the Revolution. 'Although the Revolution settlement placed some limits on the prerogative power of the Crown and established the political importance of Parliament', writes H. T. Dickinson, 'it did not show how Crown and Parliament were to co-operate harmoniously and effectively' (*Liberty and Property* (1977), p. 94). The conflict between the Country opposition in Parliament and the King and his ministers was an attempt to define the nature of the relationship, because what had been enshrined in 1689 in the Bill of Rights was in many ways only provisional. To complaints over William's reluctance to disband the army were added complaints about the lavish grants of land he had made to his Dutch favourites and to the Earl of Portland, Hans Willem Bentinck, in particular, from the forfeited estates of Irish rebels. So unpopular had the Dutch become by 1700 that the House of Commons resolved that the King should remove all foreigners from his councils.

These grumblings came to a head with the publication of John Tutchin's poem, *The Foreigners*, a particularly fine example of English xenophobia which made good use of the type of biblical allegory to be found in *Absalom and Achitophel*. This time, however, Bentinck was cast in the leading role which Shaftesbury had occupied in Dryden's poem:

These are the Vermin do our State molest;
Eclipse our Glory, and disturb our Rest.

> *BENTIR* in the Inglorious Roll the first,
> *Bentir* to this and future Ages curst,
> Of mean Descent, yet insolently proud,
> Shun'd by the Great, and hated by the Crowd;
> Who neither Blood nor Parentage can boast,
> And what he got the *Jewish* Nation lost:
> By lavish Grants whole Provinces he gains,
> Made forfeit by the *Jewish* Peoples Pains;
> Till angry *Sanhedrims* such Grants resume,
> And from the Peacock take each borrow'd Plume.
> Why should the *Gibeonites* our Land engross,
> And aggrandize their Fortunes with our loss?
> Let them in foreign States proudly command,
> They have no Portion in the Promis'd Land,
> Which immemorially has been decreed
> To be the Birth-right of the *Jewish* Seed.

John Tutchin, *The Foreigners* (1700), pp. 6–7

Tutchin's was a peculiarly nasty little-Englander poem which, in calling for Bentinck's downfall, made no apology for blaming foreigners, including the Scots, for everything which was wrong with English society. Although support for the King himself was carefully endorsed in *The Foreigners*, it also assumed a radical position on the question of the succession, hinting darkly not only that power ultimately lay with the people, as Locke had suggested, but also that a republic might be the best solution to the nation's present difficulties:

> When no Successor to the Crown's in sight,
> The Crown is certainly the Peoples Right.
> If Kings are made the People to enthral,
> We had much better have no King at all:
> But Kings, appointed for the Common Good,
> Always as Guardians to their People stood.
> And Heaven allows the People sure a Power
> To chuse such Kings as shall not them devour:
> They know full well what best will serve themselves,
> How to avoid the dang'rous Rocks and Shelves.
> Unthinking *Israel!* Ah henceforth beware
> How you entrust this faithless Wanderer!

He who another Kingdom can divide,
May set your Constitution soon aside,
And o'er your Liberties in Triumph ride.
Support your Rightful Monarch and his Crown,
But pull this proud, this croaking Mortal down.

John Tutchin, *The Foreigners* (1700), pp. 9–10

Although it is of interest in its own right, *The Foreigners* is much better known on account of Defoe's famous response, *The True-Born Englishman*, which, in the course of demolishing both Tutchin and his racist thesis, strikingly reviewed what had taken place since the Revolution:

Unhappy *England*, hast thou none but such,
To plead thy Scoundrel Cause against the Dutch?
This moves their Scorn, and not their Indignation;
He that Lampoons the Dutch, Burlesques the Nation.
The meanest *English* Plowman studies Law,
And keeps thereby the Magistrates in Awe:
Will boldly tell them what they ought to do,
And sometimes publish their Omissions too.
Their Liberty and Property's so dear,
They scorn their Laws or Governors to fear:
So bugbear'd with the Name of Slavery,
They can't submit to their own Liberty.
Restraint from Ill is Freedom to the Wise;
But Englishmen *do all Restraint despise.*
Slaves to the Liquor, Drudges to the Pots,
The Mob are Statesmen, and their Statesmen Sots.
Their Governors they count such dangerous things,
That 'tis their custom to affront their Kings:
So jealous of the Power their Kings possess'd,
They suffer neither Power nor Kings to rest.
The Bad with Force they eagerly subdue;
The Good with constant Clamours they pursue:
And did King Jesus reign, they'd murmur too.
A discontented Nation, and by far
Harder to rule in Times of Peace than War:
Easily set together by the Ears,
And full of causeless Jealousies and Fears:

Apt to revolt, and willing to rebel,
And never are contented when they're well.
No Government cou'd ever please them long,
Cou'd tye their Hands, or rectify their Tongue.
In this to Ancient Israel *well compar'd,*
Eternal Murmurs are among them heard.
    It was but lately that they were opprest,
Their Rights invaded, and their Laws supprest:
When nicely tender of their Liberty,
Lord! what a Noise they made of Slavery.
In daily Tumults show'd their Discontent;
Lampoon'd their King, and mock'd his Government.
And if in Arms they did not first appear,
'Twas want of Force, and not for want of Fear.
In humbler Tones than *English* us'd to do,
At Foreign Hands for Foreign Aid they sue.
    William *the Great Successor of* Nassau,
Their Prayers heard, and their Oppressions saw:
He saw and sav'd them: God and Him they prais'd;
To This their Thanks, to That their Trophies rais'd.
But glutted with their own Felicities,
They soon their New Deliverer despise;
Say all their Prayers back, their Joy disown,
Unsing their Thanks, and pull their Trophies down:
Their Harps of Praise are on the Willows hung;
For Englishmen *are ne're contented long.*

    Daniel Defoe, *The True-Born Englishman* (1700), pp. 39–42

What is of great interest about this exchange is that it is between Whigs: in the end, the Revolution Settlement had caused the Whigs to fall out among themselves, as rival versions of Whig ideology emerged to complicate the political situation. Although some Whigs were more or less happy with the consequences of the Revolution, others felt that the settlement had not been radical enough. Tutchin with his insistence that it was better to have 'no King at all' than one who would endanger the freedom of the people was apparently one of the latter. Defoe, on the other hand, as the King's unofficial apologist, supported those Whigs who remained in William's councils.

    To complicate matters still further, each accused the other of apostasy. To oppose the Court on such issues as the standing army and the grants to William's Dutch favourites, the radical Whigs had formed an *ad hoc* alliance with Country Tories, therefore they were accused by the ministerial Whigs of defecting to the Tory party. The radical Whigs, in turn, derided their ministerial counterparts for upholding the royal prerogative. John Toland accounted for this by arguing that it was the legacy of the malicious policies of Charles II, who had deliberately stimulated the growth of political parties by encouraging divisions within the nation at large. This was the art of governing by parties and its evil influence had survived the Revolution, even though

> the King fell in heartily with the Public Interest, his new Ministers serv'd him faithfully for a considerable Time, and all our Affairs took a better Face both at Home and Abroad, by Land and Sea. But see the Instability of human Councils, som of those surly Whigs grew by degrees the most pliant Gentlemen imaginable, they cou'd think no revenue too great for the King nor would suffer his Prerogative to be lessen'd, they were on frivolous pretences for keeping up a Standing Army to our further Peril and Charge, they fill'd all Places in their disposal with their own Creatures, combin'd together for their common Impunity, whoever found fault with their Conduct they represented him as an Enemy to the Gover[n]ment, and even oppos'd the best of Laws, lest the Torys, as they said, shou'd partake of the Benefit. Surely these Gentlemen, if it were in their Power, wou'd not suffer the Sun to shine on any but themselves and their Faction. But as this Language, this Partiality, this Conduct, were directly contrary to the Principles and Practices of the Whigs (and the Torys themselves will do Justice to the old Whigs) so these Apostates were abandon'd by their former Friends, and left to the support of their own Interest, which appear'd to be so very little with any Party that the King did wisely cashier them.

John Toland, *The Art of Governing by Partys* (1701), pp. 47–8

There were a number of reasons why the King decided to change his ministers, but perhaps the principal consideration was the death on 30 July 1700 of Princess Anne's son, the Duke of Gloucester. Queen Mary had died childless in 1694 and William had not remarried. As long as his sister-in-law Anne had heirs, there was no real problem as far as the safety of the Protestant succession was concerned. But none of Anne's offspring had survived childhood, and now the question of the succession was again of the first significance. If William died first, he would be succeeded by Princess Anne. But then what? And what would happen if Anne pre-deceased him?

At the Revolution it had not appeared to be a problem. In 1689 it had reasonably been assumed that between them James II's Protestant daughters would provide for a Protestant dynasty. But in the event neither Mary nor Anne had managed to produce an heir. The King's thoughts turned yet again to the safety of the Protestant succession. Legislation to make this secure required the co-operation of a majority in the House of Commons, so William entered negotiations with leaders of the Country opposition, summoned a new Parliament and on 3 March 1701 the House of Commons passed a resolution

> That, for the preserving the Peace and Happiness of this Kingdom, and the Security of the Protestant Religion by Law established, it is absolutely necessary, a further Declaration be made of the Limitation and Succession of the Crown in the Protestant line, after his Majesty and the Princess [Anne], and the Heirs of their Bodies respectively [. . . and] that further Provision be first made for the Security of the Rights and Liberties of the People.
>
> *Journals of the House of Commons*, XIII, 375–6

The Act of Settlement entailed the Crown after the death of Princess Anne and her heirs in the House of Hanover – the nearest Protestant heirs to the throne – and so William's wishes were fulfilled.

It is significant, however, that, in the wording of the Commons' resolution, the issue of limitation was given precedence over the question of the succession. The 'further Provision' made in the Act of Settlement 'for the Security of the Rights and Liberties of the People' amounted to little short of a revision of the Revolution Settlement itself. Not only would any future monarch have to be at least nominally Anglican, he would not be allowed to 'go out of the dominions of England, Scotland, or Ireland, without the consent of Parliament'. Other clauses prohibited foreigners, placemen, and pensioners from being Members of Parliament. These restrictions were felt by some to be excessive, and advice was offered to the House of Commons in verse:

> The limitation of the Crown
>   Is your Immediate care,
> If your *Wise Articles* go down,
> Your Power will be so Lawless grown,
>   'Tis no matter who's the Heir.
>
> Did we for this depose our Prince,
>   And Liberty assume,
> That you should with our Laws dispense,
> Commit Mankind without Offence,
>   And Govern in his room?
>
> You shou'd find out some other word
>   To give the Crowns *Accepter*,
> To call him King wou'd be absurd,
> For tho' he'l seem to wear the Sword,
>   'Tis You have got the S[c]epter.
>
> And now your wrath is smoking hot
>   Against the *Kent* Petition,
> No man alive can tell for what
> But telling Truths which pleas'd you not,
>   And taxing your Discretion.
>
> If you those Gentlemen detain
>   By your unbounded Power,
> 'Tis hop'd you'l never more complain
> Of Bishops in King *James*'s Reign,
>   Sent blindly to the *Tower*.
>
> A strange Memorial too there came,
>   Your Members to affront,
> Which told you Truths you dare not name
> And so the Paper scap'd the Flame,
>   Or else it had been burnt.

Some said the Language was severe,
    And into Passion flew,
Some too began to curse and swear,
And call'd the Author *Mutinere*,
    But all men said 'Twas True.

But oh! the Consternation now
    In which you all appear!
'Tis plain from whence your terrours flew,
For had your guilt been less you knew,
    So would have been your fear.

[Daniel Defoe?], 'Ye True-Born Englishmen
proceed' (1701), pp. [2–3]

The conduct of the House of Commons in the aftermath of the passing of the Act of Settlement was scarcely calculated to allay such misgivings. The entailing of the Crown in the Protestant line was not the only precaution that William had taken to secure his position. Hanging over Europe for many years had been the question of what would happen on the death of the sickly Emperor of Spain, Charles II. Like William, he was childless. If any major power were to inherit the whole of the Spanish Empire, the balance of power in Europe, which William had striven all his life to maintain, would be at an end.

After the inconclusive but costly Nine Years War Louis XIV was prepared to negotiate. Partition was clearly the solution, and so William and Louis drew up a secret treaty in 1698 which would have given Spain itself and most of its overseas Empire to Joseph Ferdinand of Bavaria. Unfortunately, Joseph Ferdinand promptly died. A second Partition Treaty was concluded in March 1700 which divided the Spanish Empire between the sons of the main claimants, the Emperor Leopold of Austria, and Louis XIV himself. However, Charles II of Spain thought he would have a say in who should inherit his possessions. He made a will leaving the entire Spanish Empire to Louis' grandson, Philip of Anjou, on the condition that, if it did not remain intact, then it should go to someone else. Charles II died in November 1700, Louis XIV repudiated the Second Partition Treaty and accepted his will, and his grandson was declared Philip V of Spain.

All this occurred before the passing of the Act of Settlement. Control over foreign policy had always been an undisputed part of the King's prerogative, but in April 1701 four of the King's former ministers, including Bentinck, were impeached by the House of Commons for their involvement in the negotiation and signing of the secret Partition Treaties with France. The impeachment of ministers who had been acting on William's orders was yet another challenge to the traditional authority of the Crown.

The Partition Treaties had already been overtaken by events; on the grounds that it had not been consulted, the House of Commons was objecting to their mere existence. But when Louis decided to accept Charles II's will and take the step of occupying fortresses in the Spanish Netherlands, he made another major continental war a virtual certainty. Tempers were already running high when a petition was presented to the House of Commons from the county of Kent which demanded that immediate preparations for war should be made in view of 'the dangerous Estate of this Kingdom and of all *Europe*'. The Commons did not take kindly to such advice, and the five Kentish Petitioners were summarily imprisoned.

It was at this point that Defoe entered the fray with a letter addressed to the Speaker of the House of Commons and signed 'LEGION: for we are MANY'. As well as calling for the release of the Kentish Petitioners, Defoe's so-called *Legion-Letter* listed a series of demands to do with foreign policy among which were the following:

> 4. That the growing Power of *France* be taken into Consideration; the Succession of the Emperor to the Crown of *Spain* supported, our *Protestant* Neighbours protected, as the true Interest of *England*, and the *Protestant Religion* requires.
>
> 5. That the *French* King be obliged to quit *Flanders*, or that his Majesty be addressed to declare War against him.
>
> 6. That *suitable Supplies* be granted to his Majesty, for the putting all these necessary Things in Execution, and that care be taken, that such Taxes as are raised, may be more equally assessed and collected, and scandalous Deficiencies prevented.

Daniel Defoe, [Legion's Memorial] (1701), p. 4

The release of the Kentish Petitioners quickly followed Defoe's spirited intervention, but the session which had provided for the

Protestant succession petered out with the two Houses of Parliament still in open dispute over the impeachments.

However, the Commons' high-handed treatment of the Whig Lords prompted the first political pamphlet to appear from the pen of Jonathan Swift. *A Discourse of the Contests and Dissentions Between the Nobles and the Commons in Athens and Rome With the Consequences they had upon both those States* defended the impeached Lords by drawing ingenious parallels between political proceedings in classical times and the England of 1701. With Parliament in recess, Swift professed

> to hope, that during this lucid Interval, the Members retired to their Homes, may suspend a while their *acquired Complexions*, and taught by the Calmness of the Scene and the Season, reassume the native sedateness of their Temper. If this should be so, it would be wise in them, as individual and private Mortals, to look back a little upon the Storms they have *raised*, as well as those they have *escaped*: To reflect, that they have been Authors of a new and wonderful Thing in *England*, which is, for a House of Commons to lose the universal Favour of the Numbers they represent; To observe, how those whom they thought fit to persecute for Righteousness sake, have been openly caress'd by the People; and to remember how themselves sat in fear of their Persons from popular Rage. Now, if they would know the Secret of all this unpresidented Proceeding in their Masters; they must not impute it to their Freedom in Debate, or declaring their Opinions; but to that unparliamentary Abuse of setting Individuals upon their Shoulders, who were hated by God and Man. For, it seems, the Mass of the People, in such Conjunctures as this, have opened their Eyes, and will not endure to be governed by *Clodius* and *Curios* at the Head of their *Myrmidons*, tho' these be ever so numerous, and composed of their own Representatives.
>
> This Aversion of the People to the late Proceedings of the Commons, is an Accident, that if it last a while, might be improved to good Uses for setting the Balance of Power a little more upon an Equality, than their late Measures seem to promise or admit. This Accident may

be imputed to two Causes. The first, is an universal Fear and Apprehension of the Greatness and Power of *France*, whereof the People in general seem to be very much and justly possess'd, and therefore cannot but resent to see it in so critical a Juncture, wholly laid aside by their Ministers, the Commons. The other Cause, is a great Love and Sense of Gratitude in the People towards their present King, grounded upon a long Opinion and Sense of his Merit, as well as Concessions to all their reasonable Desires; so that it is for some time they have begun to say, and to fetch Instances where he has in many things been hardly used. How long these Humours may last, (the Passions are momentary, and especially those of a Multitude) or what Consequences they may produce, a little time may discover. But whenever it comes to pass, that a popular Assembly, free from such obstructions, and already possess'd of more Power, than an equal Balance will allow, shall continue to think they have not enough, but by cramping the Hand that holds the Balance, and by Impeachments or Dissensions with the Nobles, endeavour still for more; I cannot possibly see in the common course of things, how the same Causes can produce different Effects and Consequences among us, than they did in *Greece* and *Rome*.

Jonathan Swift, *A Discourse of the Contests and Dissentions* (1701), pp. 58–9

Although Swift's polemic often distorts or misrepresents Greek and Roman history to force analogies with events in contemporary England, his pamphlet draws attention in a striking way to the painful reality of the working out of the Revolution Settlement and the current uncertainty about the relationship between King and Parliament.

By the time Swift's *Discourse* was published in October 1701, however, it too had been overtaken by events. The aim of the Grand Alliance of Austria, England and Holland, signed the previous month, was, in effect, to force Louis to recognise the necessity of a partition of the Spanish Empire or, as the actual wording put it, to obtain 'a just and reasonable satisfaction' for the Austrian Emperor. James II died in exile a few weeks later and Louis responded by recognising his son as James III of England, in direct contravention of the terms of the Treaty of Ryswick.

The safety of the Protestant succession was still very much on the minds of William and his subjects therefore, when the King mounted his horse at Hampton Court to go for a ride on 20 February 1702. Just over a fortnight later he was dead. A fall from his horse, when it (apparently) stumbled over a mole-hill, resulted in the broken collar-bone which brought on a sudden decline and William's unexpected demise. The events of the previous eighteen months had brought Europe to the brink of another war, while at home Toland's attempt to expose what he called the art of governing by parties had failed to produce the desired effect. 'This is the true spring of all those pernicious Divisions, names of distinction, Parties, Factions, Clubs, and Cabals, which have ever since distracted, torn, and very nigh consum'd us', he wrote about Charles II. 'High and Low Churchmen, Conformists and Fanaticks, Whigs and Tories, Loyalists and Rebels, Patriots and Courtiers, with the like opprobrious nick-names, are the abominable fruits of his Policy' (pp. 9–10). The Act of Settlement was supposed to unite the nation and put an end to Jacobitism. Instead, the political turmoil of 1701 proved to be an even stronger stimulus to party conflict.

3 The Rage of Party

Let *India* boast her Plants, nor envy we
The weeping Amber or the balmy Tree,
While by our Oaks the precious Loads are born,
And Realms commanded which those Trees adorn.
Not proud *Olympus* yields a nobler Sight,
Tho' Gods assembled grace his tow'ring Height,
Than what more humbler Mountains offer here,
Where, in their blessings, all those Gods appear.
See *Pan* with Flocks, with Fruits *Pomona* crown'd,
Here blushing *Flora* paints th'enamel'd Ground,
Here *Ceres'* Gifts in waving Prospect stand,
And nodding tempt the joyful Reaper's Hand,
Rich Industry sits smiling on the Plains,
And Peace and Plenty tell, a STUART reigns.

Alexander Pope, *Windsor-Forest* (1713), p. 2

As Jacobites toasted 'the little gentleman in black velvet' who had caused William III's horse to throw its rider with such fatal consequences, steps were being taken not only to ensure the peaceful accession of Queen Anne but the continuation of the policies of her brother-in-law. Parliament assembled on the very day of the King's death, 8 March 1702, when both Houses presented addresses expressing their loyalty to the new monarch, and their desire to secure the safety of the Protestant succession by force of arms. In her first speech to Parliament, Queen Anne responded with assurances that, although her own heart 'was entirely *English*' – at once an echo of her father's speech on his accession in 1685 and an unmistakable allusion to the nationality of her predecessor – she intended to pursue policies which would maintain the Protestant line and at the same time reduce the exorbitant power of the France of Louis XIV.

The safeguarding of the Protestant succession in England meant that it was no longer possible to avoid declaring war over the Spanish succession and this was duly done in May 1702. Arguments about the war or, more strictly, about the conduct and conclusion of the war, were a major factor in the party strife which was such a feature of the age of Anne. There were those who, relying on the strength of the Royal Navy, advocated a 'blue-water' policy as the best method of defence, but in the early days of the reign almost everyone recognised and accepted the necessity of a continental war to prevent the French hegemony which William had struggled against for so long from becoming a reality, though Defoe's description of a Queen eager to assume the role played by her predecessor was perhaps overly optimistic:

> *Anne* like *Elisha* when just *William* went,
> Receiv'd the Mantle of his Government:
> And by Divine Concession does inherit,
> A Double Portion of his Ruling Spirit.
> The Dying Hero loaded with Renown,
> Gave her the Nations Blessing with the Crown,
> From God, the People, and the Laws her own.
> Told her that he had Orders from on High,
> To lay aside the Government and Dye:
> What he had Fought for, gave her up in Peace,
> And chear'd her Royal Heart with Prospect of Success.
> While he, who Death in all its Shapes had seen,
> With full Composure quiet and serene,
> Passive and undisorder'd at his Fate,
> Quitted the English Throne without Regret.

> Daniel Defoe, *The Mock Mourners: A Satyr by Way of Elegy on King William* (1702), pp. 7–8

William III was Defoe's hero, but, as the curious title of his poem insinuates, others had very different expectations from the King's death. Confirming yet again the massive influence of Dryden on early-eighteenth-century political poetry, one Jacobite sympathiser followed Defoe's example by alluding to *Mac Flecknoe*, with its ruling motif of succession, to supply a striking picture of Whig dismay at William's failure to complete the republican experiment allegedly embarked upon at the Revolution:

Tho' *N[assau]*'s Death has all our Measures broke,
Yet never will we bend to *A[nna]*'s Yoke.
The glorious *Revolution* was in vain,
If Monarchy once more its Rights regain.
Let all be Chaos, and Confusion all,
E're that damn'd Form of Government prevail.
O had he liv'd to Perfect his Design,
We ne're had been Subjected to her Reign,
But rooted out the *St[uar]ts* hated Line!
Howe're, since Fate has otherwise decreed,
We may on his unfinish'd Scheme proceed.
We may 'gainst Pow'r repos'd in One inveigh,
And call all Monarchy Tyrannick Sway.
We may the Praises of the *Dutch* advance,
Rail at the Arbitrary Rule of *France*,
Extol the Commonwealth in *Adria*'s Flood,
Which for ten rowling Centuries has stood.
Argue how th' *Roman*, and *Athenian* State
Were only when Republick[s] truly Great.
'Tis easy the Unreas'ning Mob to guide,
For they are always on the Factious side.
This labour'd here, 'twill be our next Resort,
To Manage and Cajole *S[ophia]*'s Court.

[William Shippen?], *Faction Display'd* (1704), pp. 8–9

This poem succeeds in drawing attention to an interesting characteristic of the party conflict of the period: each insisted on calling into question the legitimacy of the activities of the other by referring to it as 'the faction'. To the author of *Faction Display'd*, it was self-evident that the Whigs were 'the faction'. But this terminology was readily reversible. Later on in the reign, after a Tory landslide at the polls, Swift demanded 'by what Figure of Speech [the Whigs] pretend to call so great and *unforc'd* a Majority, with the Qu[een] at the Head, by the Name of *the Faction*' (*The Examiner* No. 32: 8 March 1711).

There were a number of reasons why party strife ran so high during the reign of Queen Anne. Despite the declaration of war the Jacobites were of course cock-a-hoop on William's death and hoped for great things from a Queen who was the daughter of James II. In addition to the loaded remark about her 'entirely

English' heart, Anne also contrived to give conflicting signals in her farewell speech to the old Parliament in May 1702. Although she insisted that she would be 'very careful to preserve and maintain the Act of Toleration, and to set the Minds of all My People at Quiet', this assurance was rather qualified by what followed. 'My own Principles must always keep Me entirely firm to the Interests and Religion of the Church of *England*', the Queen explained, 'and will incline Me to countenance those who have the truest Zeal to support it' (*Journals of the House of Lords*, XVII, 150).

This was what Jacobite sympathisers wanted to hear. The newly-passed Act of Settlement notwithstanding, it kept alive hopes of a Jacobite restoration on Queen Anne's death. An integral component of the doctrine of the Divine Right of Kings had been the importance of the close relationship between Church and State. By stressing the wholeheartedness of her own support for the Established Church, the Queen's speech could be taken as covert encouragement of those who believed in other parts of the creed such as indefeasible hereditary succession, passive obedience and non-resistance.

It did not take very long for High Churchmen to sound the rallying cry of 'the Church in Danger' and the issue upon which they took their stand was that of occasional conformity. Under the terms of the Test and Corporation Acts all those who wished to hold public office, at local or at national level, had first to take communion in the Church of England. This applied even after 1689. Although the Toleration Act, passed immediately after the Revolution, permitted Protestant Dissenters to attend their Meeting Houses for divine worship rather than the Established Church, the conditions laid down by the Test Act still had to be met. As a result significant numbers of Dissenters simply conformed with the letter of the law and took communion annually in the Church of England in order to qualify for public office.

The practice outraged High Churchmen like Henry Sacheverell, who preached a number of sermons on the theme of 'the Church in Danger'. In the significantly-titled *The Political Union: A Discourse Shewing the Dependance of Government on Religion In General: And of The English Monarchy on The Church of England In Particular* Sacheverell emphasised the differences between the Church of England and its rivals even after the Toleration Act,

'as it Stands upon a *Legal* Foundation, Establish'd, and Distinguish'd, from All That Confus'd Swarm of *Sectarists*, that Gather
about Its Body, not to Partake of Its Communion, but to
Disturb Its Peace' (*Political Union*, p. 48). Understandably, he
took heart from Queen Anne's stated inclination 'to countenance
those who have the truest Zeal to support it' and he singled out
the practice of occasional conformity as the greatest threat to its
security:

> If therefore We have any Concern for Our *Religion*, any
> True Allegiance for Our *Sovereign* or Regard to the Safety
> and Honour of Our *Country*, We must Watch against
> These Crafty, Faithless, and Insidious Persons, who can
> *Creep* to Our Altars, and Partake of Our Sacraments, that
> They may be *Qualify'd*, more Secretly and Powerfully to
> Undermine Us.

> Henry Sacheverell, *The Political Union* (1702), p. 61

In conclusion Sacheverell transmogrified Anne's words into a
battle cry to be used against the occasional conformists. 'Any
Pretending to that Sacred and Inviolable Character of being Her
True Sons, Pillars, and Defenders, should Turn Such *Apostates* and
Renegadoes to Their *Oaths* and *Professions*', he proclaimed, 'every
Man, that Wishes Its Welfare, ought to Hang out the *Bloody Flag*,
and *Banner* of Defiance' (*Political Union*, p. 59).

It is scarcely surprising that after such a resounding call to
arms battle was soon joined. On 1 December 1702, the day
before a bill which would have made the practice of occasional
conformity illegal was due to receive its first reading in the
House of Lords, a pamphlet appeared which bore all the marks
of being another High Church rant from the pen of Sacheverell
or one of his cronies. *The Shortest Way with the Dissenters: Or,
Proposals for the Establishment of the Church* opened with a fable
about the condition of the Church of England in 1702 after the
neglect which, it was alleged, it had suffered during the reign of
the foreign Calvinist, William III:

> SIR *Roger L'Estrange* tells us a Story in his Collection of
> Fables, of the Cock and the Horses. The Cock was
> gotten to Roost in the Stable, among the Horses, and

there being no Racks, or other Conveniences for him, it seems, he was forc'd to roost upon the Ground; the Horses jostling about for Room, and putting the Cock in Danger of his Life, he gives them this grave Advice, *Pray Gentlefolks let us stand still, for fear we should tread upon one another.*

There are some People in the World, who now they are *unpearch'd*, and reduc'd to an Equality with other People, and under strong and very just Apprehensions of being farther treated as they deserve, begin with *Æsop's* Cock, to preach up Peace, and Union, and the Christian Duties of Moderation, forgetting, that when they had the Power in their Hands, those Graces were Strangers in their Gates.

It is now near fourteen Years that the Glory and Peace of the purest and most flourishing Church in the World has been eclips'd, buffeted, and disturb'd by a sort of Men, who God, in his Providence has suffer'd to insult over her, and bring her down; these have been the Days of her Humiliation and Tribulation: She has born with an invincible Patience, the Reproach of the Wicked, and God has at last heard her Prayers, and deliver'd her from the Oppression of the Stranger.

And now they find their Day is over, their Power gone, and the Throne of this Nation posses'd by a Royal, *English*, True, and ever Constant Member of, and Friend to the Church of *England.* Now they find that they are in Danger of the Church of *England's* just Resentments; now they cry out, *Peace, Union, Forbearance*, and *Charity*, as if the Church had not too long harbour'd her Enemies under her Wing, and nourish'd the viperous Brood, 'till they hiss and fly in the Face of the Mother that cherish'd them.

No, Gentlemen, the Time of Mercy is past, *your Day of Grace is over*; you should have practis'd Peace, and Moderation, and Charity, if you expected any your selves.

We have heard none of this Lesson for fourteen Years past: We have been huff'd and bully'd with your Act of Toleration; you have told us that you are the *Church establish'd by Law*, as well as others, have set up your

canting-synagogues at our Church-Doors, and the Church
and Members have been loaded with Reproaches, with
Oaths, Associations, Abjurations, and what not; where
has been the Mercy, the Forbearance, the Charity you
have shewn to *tender Consciences of the Church* of England,
that could not take Oaths *as fast as you made 'em*; that
having sworn Allegiance to their lawful and rightful
King, could not dispence with that Oath, *their King being
still alive*, and swear to your new *Hodge-podge of a* Dutch
Government? These have been turn'd out of their Livings,
and they and their Families left to starve, their Estates
double tax'd, to carry on a War they had *no Hand in*, and
you got nothing by.

[Daniel Defoe], *The Shortest Way with
the Dissenters* [1702], pp. 3–5

Couched in language calculated to express the feelings of High
Churchmen everywhere, the grievances listed in *The Shortest Way
with the Dissenters* encompassed everything which they had found
cause to resent since the Revolution. It even offered practical
measures, or 'proposals', which would have served to 'establish'
the Church of England more effectively:

> If one severe Law were made, and punctually executed,
> that whoever was found at a Conventicle, shou'd be
> banish'd the Nation, and the Preacher be hang'd, we
> should soon see an End of the Tale, they would all come
> to Church, and one Age would make us all one again.

[Daniel Defoe], *The Shortest Way with the Dissenters* (1702), p. 13

What if this was in direct contravention of the Toleration Act?
That scarcely mattered under a Queen who had publicly an-
nounced her inclination 'to countenance those who have the
truest zeal to support' the Church:

> [. . .] The Queen has promis'd them, to continue them in
> their tolerated Liberty; and has told us she will be a
> religious Observer of her Word.
> What her Majesty will do, we cannot help, but what,

as the Head of the Church, she ought to do, is another
Case: Her Majesty has promis'd to protect and defend
the Church of *England*, and if she cannot effectually do
that without the Destruction of the Dissenters, she must
of Course dispense with one Promise to comply with
another. But to answer *this Cavil more effectually:* Her
Majesty did never promise to maintain the Toleration, to
the Destruction of the Church [. . . .]

[Daniel Defoe], *The Shortest Way with
the Dissenters* (1702), pp. 13, 10

It seemed certain to contemporaries that the *Shortest Way* could
only have been written by a rabid High Churchman, and its
'proposals' appear to have received considerable popular support. But in bantering the Queen's speech the author was guilty
of seditious libel and the government was not slow to respond
to the challenge to authority which had been thrown down. A
proclamation was issued offering a reward for information
leading to the arrest of Daniel Defoe. Matters were not helped
when it was quickly discovered that the Queen's speech was not
the only thing that he had been bantering, for Defoe was himself
a Dissenter! It had all been a hoax, he explained, designed to
expose the bigotry of the High Churchmen and to demonstrate
'that when the Persecution and Destruction of the *Dissenters, the
very Thing they drive at*, is put into plain *English*, the whole Nation
will start at the Notion, and condemn the Author to be hang'd
for his Impudence' (*The Shortest Way with the Dissenters* (1703),
p. 18). To his disconcertment Defoe was very nearly proved
right. He escaped the gallows, but for writing and publishing a
seditious libel he was pilloried three times, fined 200 marks,
required to find sureties for his good behaviour for seven years
and incarcerated until all was performed.

Meanwhile, the controversy over occasional conformity continued to smoulder. Three bills introduced between 1702 and 1704
failed to become law, as the furore over the religious element of
the Revolution Settlement rekindled party strife and set the
nation ablaze. Jonathan Swift arrived in London around the
time the third bill was introduced into the Commons. 'I observed
the dogs in the streets much more contumelious and quarrel-
some than usual; and the very night before the bill went up [to

the Lords], a committee of Whig and Tory cats, had a very warm and loud debate upon the roof of our house', he wrote back to Ireland in typical style. 'But why should we wonder at that, when the very ladies are split asunder into High Church and Low, and out of zeal for religion have hardly time to say their prayers?' (*Correspondence*, I, 38–9). A few years later Swift offered this explanation of the way in which party had affected even the Church:

> Some time after the Revolution the Distinction of *High* and *Low*-Church came in, which was rais'd by the Dissenters, in order to break the Church Party, by dividing the Members into *High* and *Low*; and the Opinion rais'd, That the *High* join'd with the Papists, inclin'd the *Low* to fall in with the Dissenters.

> Jonathan Swift, *The Examiner* No. 44: 31 May 1711

By their very nature High Churchmen, jealous of the establishment in Church and State and, by implication, supporters of the doctrines of passive obedience and non-resistance, if not indefeasible hereditary right itself, tended to be Tories. The Whigs, on the other hand, with their insistence that princes could be replaced if they failed to govern within the terms of the (unwritten) constitution, tended not only to be Low Churchmen, but to support the claims of Protestant Dissenters to equality before the law:

> Whoever formerly profess'd himself to approve the *Revolution*, to be against the *Pretender*, to justify the Succession in the House of *Hannover*, to think the *British* Monarchy not absolute, but limited by Laws, which the Executive Power could not dispense with, and to allow an Indulgence to Scrupulous Consciences; such a Man was content to be called a *Whig*. On t'other side, whoever asserted the Queen's Hereditary Right; that the Persons of Princes were Sacred; their lawful Authority not to be resisted on any Pretence; nor even their Usurpations, without the most extream Necessity: That Breaches in the Succession were highly dangerous; that *Schism* was a great Evil, both in it self and its

Consequences; that the Ruin of the *Church*, would probably be attended with that of the *State*; that no Power should be trusted with those who are not of the Establish'd Religion; such a Man was usually call'd a *Tory*. Now, tho' the Opinions of both these are very consistent, and I really think are maintain'd at present by a great Majority of the Kingdom; yet, according as Men apprehend the Danger greater, either from the *Pretender* and his Party, or from the Violence and Cunning of *other Enemies* to the Constitution; so their common Discourses and Reasonings, turn either to the first or second Set of these Opinions I have mention'd, and are consequently styl'd either *Whigs* or *Tories*. Which is, as if two *Brothers* Apprehended their House would be set upon, but disagreed about the Place from whence they thought the *Robbers* would come, and therefore would go on different sides to defend it.

Jonathan Swift, *The Examiner* No. 44: 31 May 1711

Swift managed to resist what was for him the severe temptation to enter the controversy over occasional conformity while the successive bills which would have made the practice illegal were being headed off in Parliament. But by 1708, with the government becoming ever more dependent for support upon the Whigs, it was being rumoured that the Test Act itself was in danger of being repealed. That would have been too much, and so in his best ironic manner Swift wrote 'AN ARGUMENT To prove, That The Abolishing of CHRISTIANITY IN *ENGLAND*, May, as Things now stand, be attended with some Inconveniences, and perhaps not produce those many Good Effects propos'd thereby':

NOR do I think it wholly groundless, or my Fears altogether imaginary, that the Abolishing of Christianity may perhaps bring the CHURCH in Danger, or at least put the Senate to the Trouble of another Securing Vote. I desire I may not be mistaken; I am far from presuming to affirm, or to think, that the CHURCH is in Danger at present, or as Things now stand; but we know not how soon it may be so, when the Christian Religion is repealed. As plausible as this Project seems, there may be a dangerous Design lurk under it; Nothing can be more notorious, than that the *Atheists, Deists, Socinians, Anti-Trinitarians*, and other Subdivisions of Free-Thinkers, are Persons of little Zeal for the present Ec[c]lesiastical Establishment: Their declared Opinion is for repealing the Sacramental Test; they are very indifferent with regard to Ceremonies; nor do they hold the *Jus Divinum* of Episcopacy. Therefore this may be intended as one Politick Step towards altering the Constitution of the Church Established, and setting up *Presbytery* in the stead; which I leave to be further considered by those at the Helm.

IN the last Place, I think nothing can be more plain, than that by this Expedient, we shall run into the Evil we chiefly pretend to avoid; and that the Abolishment of the Christian Religion, will be the readiest Course we can take to introduce Popery. And I am the more inclined to this Opinion, because we know it hath been the constant Practice of the *Jesuits* to send over Emissaries, with Instructions to personate themselves Members of the several prevailing Sects amongst us. So it is recorded, that they have at sundry Times appeared in the Guise of *Presbyterians, Anabaptists, Independents* and *Quakers*, according as any of these were most in Credit; So, since the Fashion hath been taken up of exploding Religion, the *Popish* Missionaries have not been wanting to mix with the Free-Thinkers [. . .] the Fact is beyond Dispute, and the Reasoning they proceed by is right: For supposing Christianity to be extinguished, the People will never be at Ease till they find out some other Method of Worship; which will as infallibly produce Superstition, as this will end in *Popery*.

AND therefore, if notwithstanding all I have said, it still be thought necessary to have a Bill brought in for repealing Christianity; I would humbly offer an Amendment; that instead of the Word Christianity, may be put Religion in general, which I conceive will much better answer all the good Ends proposed by the Projectors of it. For, as long as we leave in being, a God and his Providence, with all the necessary Consequences which curious and inquisitive Men will be apt to draw from such Premises, we do not strike at the Root of the Evil, although we should ever so effectually annihilate the present Scheme of the Gospel. For, of what use is Freedom of Thought, if it will not produce Freedom of Action, which is the sole End, how remote soever in Appearance, of all Objections against Christianity?

Jonathan Swift, *An Argument against Abolishing Christianity* (1717), pp. 33–6

In the hands of a reductive satirist like Swift Christianity equates with the allegedly primitive doctrine of the Church of England, while both Roman Catholicism and Protestant Nonconformity are presented as entirely different religions. From this reduced perspective to repeal the Test and Corporation Acts would therefore be the equivalent of repealing the Christian religion itself, as Swift suggests. It is telling that others were prepared to make much the same connection between religion and politics without irony, without satire. On 5 November 1709 – the anniversary of not only the Gunpowder Plot but the landing of William of Orange in England – Henry Sacheverell preached his most notorious sermon in St Paul's Cathedral on the text 'In perils among false brethren' (2 Corinthians 11. v. 26).

What is remarkable about the performance for which Sacheverell was impeached, found guilty of seditious libel and banned from preaching for three years is not so much the originality of its ideas or their exposition – they were, after all, little more than a set of indifferently expressed commonplaces – as the clear indication it gives of the survival, against all the odds, of the panoply of Divine Right doctrines which should have perished at the Revolution:

Our *Constitution* both in *Church*, and *State* has been so admirably *Contriv'd*, with that *Wisdom*, *Weight*, and *Sagacity*, and the *Temper*, and *Genius* of each, so exactly *Suited*, and *Modell'd* to the *Mutual Support*, and *Assistance* of One another, that 'tis hard to say, whether the *Doctrins* of the *Church of England* contribute *more* to *Authorize*, and *Enforce* Our *Civil Laws*, or Our *Laws* to *Maintain*, and *Defend* the *Doctrins* of Our *Church*. The Natures of Both are so

nicely *Correspondent*, and so happily *Intermixt*, that 'tis
almost impossible to offer a *Violation*, to the *One*,
without *Breaking* in upon the *Body* of the *Other*. So that
in all those *Cases* before-mention'd, whosoever *Presumes*
to *Innovate*, *Alter*, or *Misrepresent* any *Point* in the *Articles*
of the *Faith* of our *Church*, ought to be *Arraign'd* as a
Traytor to our *State*; *Heterodoxy* in the *Doctrins* of the *One*,
Naturally producing, and almost *Necessarily Inferring Rebellion*, and *High-Treason* in the *Other*, and consequently a
Crime that concerns the *Civil Magistrate*, as much to
Punish, and *Restrain*, as the *Ecclesiastical*. However this
Assertion at first View may look like an *High-flown
Paradox*, the Proof of it will fully appear in a few
Instances. The *Grand Security* of our *Government*, and the
very *Pillar* upon which it *stands*, is founded upon the
steady Belief of the *Subject's Obligation* to an *Absolute*, and
Unconditional Obedience to the *Supream Power*, in *All* Things
Lawful, and the utter *Illegality* of *Resistance* upon any *Pretence*
whatsoever. But this *Fundamental Doctrin*, notwithstanding it's [*sic*] *Divine Sanction* in the *Express Command* of *God*
in *Scripture*, and without which, it is impossible any
Government of any *Kind*, or *Denomination* in the World,
should *subsist* with Safety, and which has been so long
the *Honourable*, and *Distinguishing Characteristic* of *Our
Church*, is now, it seems, quite *Exploded*, and *Redicul'd* [*sic*]
out of Countenance, as an *Unfashionable, Superannuated*,
nay (which is more wonderful) as a *Dangerous Tenet*,
utterly *Inconsistent* with the *Right, Liberty*, and *Property* of
the PEOPLE; who, as our *New Preachers*, and *New
Politicians* teach us, (I suppose by a *New*, and *Unheard* of
Gospel, as well as *Laws*) have in Contradiction to *Both*, the
Power Invested in *Them*, the Fountain and *Original* of it,
to *Cancel* their *Allegiance* at pleasure, and call their
Sovereign to account for *High-Treason* against his *Supream
Subjects* forsooth; nay to *Dethrone*, and *Murder* Him for a
Criminal, as they did the *Royal Martyr* by a *Judiciary*
Sentence. And what is almost Incredible, presume to
make their *Court* to their *Prince*, by maintaining such
Anti-monarchical Schemes. But, God be Thanked! neither
the Constitution of Our *Church* or *State*, is so far *Alter'd*,
but that by the *Laws of Both*, (*still* in Force, and which I

hope *for ever* will be) these *Damnable Positions*, let 'em come either from *Rome*, or *Geneva*, from the *Pulpit*, or the *Press*, are condemn'd for *Rebellion*, and *High-Treason*.

Henry Sacheverell, *The Perils of False Brethren, both in Church, and State* (1709), pp. 18–21

In reasserting the doctrines of passive obedience and non-resistance it was apparent that, however much lip-service he paid to it, Sacheverell had preached against the Revolution. He was the oath-swearing, crypto-Jacobite *par excellence* and therefore he had to be challenged. ' 'Tis not *Sacheverell* that is to be try'd', Defoe pointed out. ' '[T]is not one Farthing Matter what the *House* [of Lords] did with him, a poor contemptible noisie Body'. Much more weighty matters were at stake. 'Here the Validity of the Revolution will be try'd', Defoe explained. 'Here the present Constitution is to be try'd, and the *Lords* are to give Sentence upon it'. What Defoe wanted was a judgement which would finally signal the victory of Revolution Principles. Were this to happen, then the 'Principles of *Jacobitism* would wither away, for Want of the Vital Moisture they receive from these Notions' (*The Review*, VI, 479, 542–3, 475).

The conviction of Sacheverell was an important stage in the continuing process of safeguarding and legitimising the Revolutionary regime, but, despite Defoe's optimism, it was insufficient on its own to settle matters. The Act of Union with Scotland which brought Great Britain into being in 1707 ensured that Queen Anne would have the same successor north and south of the border and effectually closed England's 'postern gate' to the Pretender. And yet the Protestant succession still had to be defended by force of arms virtually throughout the reign. Together with the religious strife which divided English society in these years attitudes towards the War of the Spanish Succession ensured that the conflict between the Whig and Tory parties which was becoming a constant feature of the political life of the nation was sustained at a high temperature. Thanks to the military genius of the Duke of Marlborough, the allies had won resounding victories in the field against the armies of Louis XIV at Blenheim (1704), Ramillies (1706), Oudenarde (1708), and Malplaquet (1709). But peace had not yet broken out when Sacheverell preached his sermon.

This was the cause of some anxiety and no little resentment to the country gentlemen whose taxes paid for the war. War-weariness was rife even before the Battle of Malplaquet (which took place on 11 September 1709), and it was hardly surprising that Marlborough was accused of prolonging the war for his own ends. Louis XIV had opened peace negotiations the previous spring, prepared to make immense concessions to the allies, including the surrender of the entire Spanish Empire. But this wasn't good enough for rampant allied plenipotentiaries. They required Louis' compliance with the outrageous Thirty-seventh of the 'Preliminary Articles' with which he was presented as an ultimatum in May. This declared that the ending of hostilities was conditional on the surrender of the Spanish monarchy by Louis' grandson, Philip V, within two months of the signing of a peace treaty. If this did not take place, then war could begin again with the allies in the advantageous position they would be in after the surrendering by the French of fortresses they presently held in the Spanish Netherlands.

British public opinion anticipated the ending of the war despite the arrogance of the 'Preliminary Articles', and Whig propagandists made the most of the opportunity to reply to the repeated allegations from the Tories that Marlborough was reluctant to make peace:

> The Approach of a Peace strikes a Pannick thro' our Armies, tho' that of a Battle could never do it, and they almost repent of their Bravery, that made such hast to humble themselves and the *French* King. The Duke of *Marlborough*, tho' otherwise the greatest General of the Age, has plainly shown himself unacquainted with the Arts of Husbanding a War [. . .] For the Command of General in *Flanders* hath been ever look'd upon as a Provision for Life. For my Part, I can't see how his Grace can answer it to the World, for the great Eagerness he hath shown to send a Hundred Thousand of the bravest Fellows in *Europe* a begging. But the private Gentlemen of the Infantry will be able to shift for themselves; a brave Man can never starve in a Country stock'd with Hen-roosts. *There is not a Yard of Linen*, says my honoured Progenitor Sir *John Falstaff*, *in my whole Company*; *but as for that*, says this worthy Knight, *I am in*

no great pain, we shall find Shirts on every Hedge. There is
another Sort of Gentlemen whom I am much more
concern'd for, and that is, the ingenious Fraternity of
which I have the Honour to be a unworthy Member; I
mean the *News Writers* of *Great Britain*, whether *Post-Men*
or *Post-Boys*, or by what other Name or Title soever
dignified or distinguish'd. The Case of these Gentlemen
is, I think, more hard than that of the Soldiers, consider-
ing that they have taken more Towns, and fought more
Battles. They have been upon Parties and Skirmishes,
when our Armies have lain still; and given the General
Assault to many a Place, when the Besiegers were quiet
in their Trenches. They have made us Masters of several
strong Towns many Weeks before our Generals could
do it; and compleated Victories, when our greatest
Captains have been glad to come off with a drawn Battle
[. . .] It is impossible for this ingenious Sort of Men to
subsist after a Peace: Every one remembers the Shifts
they were driven to in the Reign .of King *Charles* the
Second, when they could not furnish out a single Paper
of News, without lighting up a Comet in *Germany*, or a
Fire in *Moscow*. There scarce appear'd a Letter without a
Paragraph on an Earthquake. Prodigies were grown so
familiar, that they had lost their Name, as a great Poet
[Dryden] of that Age has it.

[Joseph Addison], *The Tatler* No. 18: 19–21 May 1709

Addison's badinage would have served its turn well enough, had
Louis XIV not rejected the peace preliminaries. Even after a
further season of fruitless campaigning, culminating in the
bloody Battle of Malplaquet, the allies still required French
acceptance of the Thirty-seventh Article of the Preliminaries at
Gertruydenberg in March 1710. 'There was scarcely anything the
Allies might not have had from France in Europe or America',
Trevelyan sagely observes, 'except the one absurdity on which
they insisted' (*England Under Queen Anne* (1930–34), III, 32).
Louis XIV was not prepared to go to war to eject his own
grandson from the Spanish monarchy which he had accepted in
his name.

Taken together, Sacheverell's impeachment and the failure to make peace were crucial factors in Queen Anne's decision to change her government. As Burnet remarked about the Ministerial Revolution of 1710, 'so sudden and so entire a change of the ministry is scarce to be found in our history' (*History of My Own Time*, VI, 10–11). The mandate for the new ministry, confirmed at the polls in October 1710, was to make peace, and Marlborough once again bore the brunt of the nation's complaints. By drawing up 'A Bill of *British* Ingratitude', and comparing it with a supposed 'Bill of *Roman* Gratitude', Swift in *The Examiner* dealt with 'one specious Objection to the late removals at Court'

> the fear of giving Uneasiness to a General, who has been long successful abroad: And accordingly, the common Clamour of Tongues and Pens for some Months past, has run against the Baseness, the Inconstancy and Ingratitude of the whole Kingdom to the Duke of *M[arlborough]*, in return of the most eminent Services that ever were perform'd by a Subject to his Country; not to be equal'd in History.

Jonathan Swift, *The Examiner* No. 17: 23 November 1710

In the event, this turned out to be only the prologue to a most vicious *ad hominem* attack on Marlborough's avarice in the form of an open letter, ostensibly to the Roman general, Crassus, but transparently addressed to the British Captain-General:

To Marcus Crassus, *Health.*

IF you apply as you ought, what I now write, you will be more oblig'd to me than to all the World, hardly excepting your Parents or your Country. I intend to tell you, without Disguise or Prejudice, the Opinion which the World has entertain'd of you: And to let you see I write this without any sort of ill Will, you shall first hear the Sentiments they have to your Advantage. No Man disputes the Gracefulness of your Person; You are allowed to have a good and clear Understanding, cultivated by the Knowledge of Men and Manners, though not by Literature. *You are no ill Orator in the Senate; you are said to excel in the Art of bridling and subduing your Anger, and stifling or concealing your*

Resentments. You have been a most successful General, of long Experience, great Conduct, and much Personal Courage. You have gain'd many important Victories for the Commonwealth, and forc'd the strongest Towns in Mesopotamia *to surrender, for which frequent* Supplications *have been decreed by the Senate. Yet with all these Qualities, and this Merit, give me leave to say, you are neither beloved by the* Patricians *or* Plebeians *at home, nor by the Officers or private Soldiers of your own Army abroad: And, do you know,* Crassus, *that this is owing to a Fault, of which you may Cure your self, by one Minute's Reflection? What shall I say? You are the richest Person in the Commonwealth; You have no Male Child, your Daughters are all Married to wealthy* Patricians; *you are far in the decline of Life; and yet you are deeply stain'd with that odious and ignoble Vice of* Covetousness: *'Tis affirm'd, that you descend even to the meanest and most scandalous Degrees of it; and while you possess so many Millions, while you are daily acquiring so many more, you are sollicitous how to save a single* Sesterce, *of which a hundred ignominious Instances are produc'd, and in all Mens Mouths [. . .]*

Instead of using the common Arguments to dissuade you from this Weakness, I will endeavour to convince you, that you are really guilty of it, and leave the Cure to your own good Sense. For perhaps, you are not yet persuaded that this is your Crime, you have probably never yet been reproach'd for it to your Face, and what you are now told, comes from One unknown, and it may be, from an Enemy. You will allow your self indeed to be prudent in the Management of your Fortunes; You are not a Prodigal, like Clodius *or* Cataline, *but surely that deserves not the Name of* Avarice. *I will inform you how to be convinced. Disguise your Person; go among the Common People in* Rome; *introduce Discourses about your self; inquire into your own Character; do the same in your Camp, walk about it in the Evening, hearken at every Tent, and if you do not hear every Mouth Censuring, Lamenting, Cursing this Vice in you, and even You for this Vice, conclude your self Innocent. If you are not yet persuaded, send for* Atticus, Servius Sulpicius, Cato *or* Brutus, *they are all your Friends; conjure them to tell you ingenuously which is your great Fault, and which they would chiefly wish you to correct; if they do not all agree in their Verdict,* in the Name of all the Gods, *you are acquitted.*

When your Adversaries reflect how far you are gone in this Vice, they are tempted to talk as if we owed our Success, not to Your Courage or Conduct, but to those Veteran *Troops you command, who are able to Conquer under* any General, *with so many brave and experienc'd Officers to lead them. Besides, we know the Consequences your Avarice hath often occasion'd. The Soldier hath been starving for Bread, surrounded with Plenty, and in an Enemies Country, but all under* Sauf-guards *and* Contributions; *which if you had sometimes pleas'd to have exchang'd for* Provisions, *might at the Expence of a few* Talents *in a Campaign, have so endear'd you to the Army, that they would have desired you to lead them to the utmost Limits of* Asia. *But you rather chose to confine your Conquests within the Fruitful Country of* Mesopotamia, *where Plenty of Money might be rais'd. How far that fatal Greediness of Gold may have influenc'd you, in breaking off the Treaty with the old* Parthian *King* Orodes [Louis XIV], *you best can tell; your Enemies charge you with it, your Friends offer nothing material in your Defence; and all agree, there is nothing so pernicious, which the Extreams of Avarice may not be able to inspire.*

The Moment you quit this Vice, you will be a truly Great Man, and still there will Imperfections enough remain to convince us, you are not a God. *Farewel.*

It was unthinkable that contemporary readers of *The Examiner* could fail to pick up Swift's pointed comparison between Crassus and Marlborough, but just in case they did he concluded with a paragraph of commentary:

Perhaps a Letter of this Nature, sent to so reasonable a Man as *Crassus*, might have put him upon *Examining* into himself, and correcting that little sordid Appetite, so utterly inconsistent with all Pretences to a *Hero*. A Youth in the heat of Blood may plead with some shew of Reason, that he is not able to subdue his Lusts; An ambitious Man may use the same Arguments for his love of Power, or perhaps other Arguments to justify it. But, Excess of Avarice hath neither of these Pleas to offer; it is not to be justified, and cannot pretend Temptation for Excuse: Whence can the Temptation come? Reason disclaims it altogether, and it cannot be said to lodge in the *Blood*, or the *Animal Spirits*. So that I conclude, *No Man of true Valour and true Understanding, upon whom this Vice has stollen unawares, when he is convinced he is guilty, will suffer it to remain in his Breast an hour.*

Jonathan Swift, *The Examiner* No. 28: 1–8 February 1711

Swift had succeeded in running through the gamut of complaints against Marlborough, not even shrinking from repeating the charge that the peace negotiations with Louis XIV had been sabotaged for personal gain. This particular issue of *The Examiner* appeared on 8 February 1711 and received the usual reply from Arthur Maynwaring in *The Medley* four days later. Within a month, however, Joseph Addison was writing a different sort of allegory about the change of ministry in a brand-new journal, *The Spectator*:

> IN one of my late Rambles, or rather Speculations, I looked into the great Hall where the Bank is kept, and was not a little pleased to see the Directors, Secretaries, and Clerks, with all the other Members of that wealthy Corporation, ranged in their several Stations, according to the Parts they act in that just and regular Oeconomy. This revived in my Memory the many Discourses which I had both read and heard concerning the Decay of Publick Credit, with the Methods of restoring it, and which, in my Opinion, have always been defective, because they have always been made with an Eyes to separate Interests, and Party Principles.
>
> The Thoughts of the Day gave my Mind Employment for the whole Night, so that I fell insensibly into a kind of Methodical Dream, which dispos'd all my Contemplations into a Vision or Allegory, or what else the Reader shall please to call it. Methoughts I returned to the Great Hall, where I had been the Morning before, but, to my Surprize, instead of the Company that I left there, I saw towards the Upper-end of the Hall, a beautiful Virgin, seated on a Throne of Gold. Her Name (as they told me) was *Publick Credit*. The Walls, instead of being adorned with Pictures and Maps, were hung with many Acts of Parliament written in Golden Letters. At the Upper-end

of the Hall was the *Magna Charta*, with the Act of Uniformity on the right Hand, and the Act of Toleration on the left. At the Lower-end of the Hall was the Act of Settlement, which was placed full in the Eye of the Virgin that sat upon the Throne. Both the Sides of the Hall were covered with such Acts of Parliament as had been made for the Establishment of publick Funds. The Lady seemed to set an unspeakable Value upon these several Pieces of Furniture, insomuch that she often refreshed her Eye with them, and often smiled with a Secret Pleasure, as she looked upon them; but, at the same time, showed a very particular Uneasiness, if she saw any thing approaching that might hurt them. She appeared indeed infinitely timorous in all her Behaviour; And, whether it was from the Delicacy of her Constitution, or that she was troubled with Vapours, as I was afterwards told by one who I found was none of her Well-wishers, she changed Colour, and startled at every thing she heard. She was likewise (as I afterwards found) a greater Valetudinarian than any I had ever met with, even in her own Sex, and subject to such Momentary Consumptions, that in the twinkling of an Eye, she would fall away from the most florid Complexion, and the most healthful State of Body, and wither into a Skeleton. Her Recoveries were often as sudden as her Decays, insomuch that she would revive in a Moment out of a wasting Distemper, into a Habit of the highest Health and Vigour.

I had very soon an Opportunity of observing these quick Turns and Changes in her Constitution [. . .] After a little Dizziness, and confused Hurry of Thought, which a Man often meets with in a Dream, methoughts the Hall was alarm'd, the Doors flew open, and there entered half a dozen of the most hideous Phantoms that I had ever seen (even in a Dream) before that Time. They came in two by two, though match'd in the most dissociable Manner, and mingled together in a kind of Dance. It would be tedious to describe their Habits and Persons, for which Reason I shall only inform my Reader that the first Couple were Tyranny and Anarchy, the second were Bigotry and Atheism, the third the

Genius of a Common-Wealth, and a young Man of about twenty two Years of Age, whose Name I could not learn [James, the Old Pretender]. He had a Sword in his right Hand, which in the Dance he often brandished at the Act of Settlement; and a Citizen, who stood by me, whisper'd in my Ear, that he saw a Spunge in his left Hand [. . .] The Reader will easily supposed, by what has been before said, that the Lady on the Throne would have been almost frighted to Distraction, had she seen but any one of these Spectres; what then must have been her Condition when she saw them all in a Body? She fainted and dyed away at the Sight
[. . .] Whilst I was lamenting this sudden Desolation that had been made before me, the whole Scene vanished: In the Room of the frightful Spectres, there now entered a second Dance of Apparitions very agreeably matched together, and made up of very amiable Phantoms. The first Pair was Liberty, with Monarchy at her right Hand: The second was Moderation leading in Religion; and the third a Person whom I had never seen [Prince George of Hanover, the Protestant heir-apparent], with the Genius of *Great Britain*. At their first Entrance the Lady reviv'd [. . .] And for my own Part I was so transported with Joy, that I awaked, tho' I must confess I would fain have fallen asleep again to have closed my Vision, if I could have done it.

[Joseph Addison], *The Spectator* No. III: 3 March 1711

By juxtaposing tyranny and anarchy with liberty and monarchy, bigotry and atheism with moderation and religion, the genius of a commonwealth with the genius of Great Britain, and the Roman Catholic Pretender to the British throne, James Stuart, with the Protestant heir-apparent, Prince George of Hanover, Addison presented a striking series of binary oppositions. He did much the same just over two years later in his political play, *Cato*, in which the eponymous defender of the Roman republic is contrasted for ideological effect with the imperial usurper, Cæsar. Liberty and virtue (rather than liberty and monarchy) are the most overworked words in the play, with Cato grieving more for the loss of Roman liberty than for the death of his son:

Alas my Friends!
Why mourn you thus? Let not a private Loss
Afflict your Hearts. 'Tis *Rome* requires our Tears.
The Mistress of the World, the Seat of Empire,
The Nurse of Heroes, the Delight of Gods,
That humbled the proud Tyrants of the Earth,
And set the Nations free, *Rome* is no more.
O Liberty! O Virtue! O my Country!

Joseph Addison, *Cato. A Tragedy* (1713), p. 53

As contemporary playgoers observed, the Whigs cheered every time liberty was mentioned as a satire on the Tories, while the Tories echoed the cheer to show that the satire was unfelt. By 1713, the word 'liberty' had been loaded with such an ideological burden that, as we shall see, it is unsafe to assume that either party had a monopoly on its use.

This was not yet the case as far as the money-market was concerned, however, and in Tory circles Addison's *Spectator* paper touched a raw nerve. As his final argument against abolishing Christianity Swift had offered his suspicion 'that in Six Months time after the Act is past for the Extirpation of the Gospel, the Bank, and *East-India* Stock, may fall at least One *per Cent*' (*An Argument against Abolishing Christianity*, p. 38). This was by no means as inconsequential a consideration as it might seem. During the Ministerial Revolution of 1710 the outgoing administration engineered a credit crisis as a last desperate attempt to hold on to office, and Addison was quite cynically drawing attention to this continuing crisis of confidence in his *Spectator* paper, the appearance of which was carefully timed to coincide with the elections for the Directors of the Bank of England. The fact that, even then, the country could in effect be held to ransom by the monied men of the City was a source of outrage to country gentlemen, and once again Swift was the principal spokesman of the landed interest.

The failure to make peace was linked to the credit crisis to form the basis of a conspiracy thesis. This conspiracy existed only in the minds of country gentlemen who paid the land tax. It was a political fiction. But it is understandable that such a connection was made, and that it was brilliantly exploited by Swift in *The Conduct of the Allies, and of the Late*

Ministry, In Beginning and Carrying on the Present War. Swift began in this way:

> *I Cannot sufficiently admire the Industry of a sort of Men, wholly out of Favour with the Prince and People, and openly professing a separate Interest from the Bulk of the Landed Men, who yet are able to raise, at this Juncture, so great a Clamour against a Peace, without offering one single Reason but what we find in their* Ballads. *I lay it down for a Maxim, That no reasonable Person, whether* Whig *or* Tory *(since it is necessary to use those foolish Terms) can be of Opinion for continuing the War, upon the Foot it now is, unless he be a Gainer by it, or hopes it may occasion some new Turn of Affairs at home, to the Advantage of his Party; or lastly, unless he be very ignorant of the Kingdom's Condition, and by what Means we have been reduced to it. Upon the two first Cases, where Interest is concerned, I have nothing to say: But as to the last, I think it highly necessary, that the Publick should be freely and impartially told what Circumstances they are in, after what Manner they have been treated by those whom they trusted so many Years with the Disposal of their Blood and Treasure, and what the Consequences of this Management are like to be upon themselves and their Posterity.*
>
> *Those who, either by Writing or Discourse, have undertaken to defend the Proceedings of the Late Ministry, in the Management of the War, and of the Treaty at* Gertruydenburg, *have spent time in celebrating the Conduct and Valour of our Leaders and their Troops, in summing up the Victories they have gained, and the Towns they have taken. Then they tell us what high Articles were insisted on by our Ministers and those of the Confederates, and what Pains both were at in persuading* France *to accept them. But nothing of this can give the least Satisfaction to the just Complaints of the Kingdom. As to the War, our Grievances are, That a greater Load has been laid on Us than was either just or necessary, or than we have been able to bear; that the grossest Impositions have been submitted to for the Advancement of private Wealth and Power, or in order to forward the more dangerous Designs of a* Faction, *to both which a Peace would have put an End; And that the Part of the War which was chiefly our Province, which would have been most beneficial to us, and destructive to the Enemy, was wholly neglected. As to a Peace, We complain of being deluded by a* Mock Treaty; *in which those who*

> *Negotiated, took care to make such Demands as they knew were impossible to be complied with, and therefore might securely press every Article as if they were in earnest.*

Jonathan Swift, *The Conduct of the Allies* (1711), Preface

The Conduct of the Allies was designed to discredit the actions of the previous government, to insinuate that there had been an understanding between former ministers and the allies to prolong the war for their mutual benefit, and to prepare the way for the revelation that negotiations between Britain and France were already on foot, contrary to the terms of the Grand Alliance, which were supposed to prevent any country from concluding a separate peace treaty with Louis XIV. The pamphlet was an enormous success. After resolutions were passed in Parliament that were strongly influenced by Swift's rhetoric, the Dutch were, in effect, rail-roaded into joining the British in ending the war.

Pope commemorated the signing of the Peace of Utrecht in 1713 in his poem, *Windsor-Forest*, which consciously imitated Virgil's *Georgics* in both theme and form. While Virgil envisaged the *pax Augusta*, Pope looked forward to a new Golden Age of peace under 'great ANNA' after the tribulations of the previous century:

> [. . .] What Tears has *Albion* shed,
> Heav'ns! what new Wounds, and how her old have bled?
> She saw her Sons with purple Deaths expire,
> Her sacred Domes involv'd in rolling Fire.
> A dreadful Series of Intestine Wars,
> Inglorious Triumphs, and dishonest Scars.
> At length great *ANNA* said – Let Discord cease!
> She said, the World obey'd, and all was *Peace*!

Alexander Pope, *Windsor-Forest* (1713), p. 14

Pope's vision embraced peace at home and an end to the rage of party. But *Windsor-Forest* is not only a poem of national reconciliation in which 'Peace and Plenty tell, a STUART reigns'. It also celebrates the dawn of British imperialism: from now on at Whitehall, Pope suggests, 'Kings shall sue, and suppliant States

be seen/Once more to bend before a *British* QUEEN' (p. 16).
Pope at once contrasts Anne with her predecessor, William III,
to the latter's detriment, reminds his readers that the reigning
monarch is a Stuart and offers a eulogy to the deity under whose
patronage the Golden Age will be restored:

> Fair *Liberty*, *Britannia*'s Goddess, rears
> Her chearful Head, and leads the golden Years.
>
> Alexander Pope, *Windsor-Forest* (1713), p. 4

   Given these conflicting political signals, it is therefore scarcely
surprising that critics have discerned Jacobite sympathies in
Pope's poem. The Peace of Utrecht may have secured Britain's
position in the early-eighteenth-century world, but the question
of succession was yet to be settled. Until a Hanoverian monarch
arrived on British soil and was safely ensconced on the throne,
arrangements for Anne's successor, despite the Act of Settlement, could only be regarded as provisional at best. Many
Jacobite sympathisers welcomed the end of the war, in fact,
seeing it as an opportunity to restore James Stuart at the eleventh
hour. Soon after Pope offered his paean to 'Sacred Peace!',
Defoe published a very different work with the sobering title, *An
Answer to a Question that No Body Thinks of, Viz. But what if the
Queen should die?* (1713). It was a very good question, too. We
must remember that no one knew how long Queen Anne would
live or what would happen on her death. The Regency Act of
1706 catered for the immediate setting up of a regency to govern
until the arrival of the new monarch, but the best-laid plans
could be disrupted and Anne persisted in her refusal to allow the
heir-apparent to reside in or even visit Britain during her
lifetime.

   There was therefore still a possibility, when Pope published
Windsor-Forest, that a Stuart would reign over Great Britain even
after the death of Queen Anne. Secret negotiations had been going
on throughout the reign, virtually without a break, between the
Court of the Pretender at St Germains and leading ministers in
England (as indeed they had ever since the Revolution). In most
instances this seems simply to have been a case of English
politicians hedging their bets, should the unlikely happen and the
Stuart line be restored to the throne. But a number of Tory

politicians were more serious in their approaches, and the Pretender was being encouraged to turn Protestant to make a reversion in his favour more acceptable to the nation at large. But to no avail. In the event George I's accession to the throne of Great Britain was accomplished without a hitch. There were then two reasons why Pope's vision of 'the golden Years' of peace under Stuart auspices remained no more than a pious hope: first, even after the conclusion of peace at Utrecht, there was plenty of life left in the party struggle which, fuelled by uncertainties over the succession, had been going on almost continuously since the 1670s; and second, with the death of Queen Anne on 1 August 1714, a Stuart reigned over Britain no longer.

4 Public Virtues, Private Vices

Or (darker Prospect! scarce one Gleam behind
Disclosing) should the broad *corruptive Plague*
Breathe from the City to the farthest Hut,
That sits serene within the Forest-Shade;
The fever'd People fire, inflame their Wants,
And their luxurious Thirst, so gathering Rage,
That, were a Buyer found, they stand *prepar'd*
To sell their Birthright for a cooling Draught.
Should *shameless Pens* for *plain Corruption* plead;
The hir'd Assassins of the Commonweal!
Deem'd the declaiming Rant of GREECE and ROME,
Should *Public Virtue* grow the *Public Scoff*,
'Till *Private*, failing, *staggers* thro' the Land.

James Thomson, *The Prospect: Being the Fifth Part of Liberty,
A Poem* (1736), p. 20

George I's peaceful accession to the throne in accordance with
the provisions of the Act of Settlement was quickly consolid-
ated by a massive handover of power to the triumphant
Whigs. The Tory party was discarded, destined to remain in
permanent opposition for several generations. Some of its leading lights, Bolingbroke and Ormonde, fled to France and
the Court of the Pretender, as proceedings within Parliament
leading to their impeachment for high treason and high crimes
and misdemeanours began in 1715. Others stayed behind, and
tried to salvage something from the political wreckage. Their
claim to be legitimate contenders for power under the Hanoverians was not helped by the Jacobite policy of direct intervention
in British politics, which allowed the Whigs to blacken the entire
Tory party with the smear of wishing to restore a Stuart to the
throne.

Jacobites there were indeed within Tory ranks, and preparations for a Jacobite invasion were proceeding apace. On 20 July 1715 George I asked Parliament for assistance in suppressing the 'Spirit of Rebellion'. Three days later the suspension of *habeas corpus* received the royal assent. Interestingly enough, *The Whole Duty of Man*, with its section on passive obedience, was also reprinted in 1715, over fifty years after its original publication. This time it was the Whig establishment which sought to remind the subject of his duty to 'the powers that be'. None of this could prevent the Earl of Mar from raising the Pretender's standard at Braemar on 6 September. Just over a month later, on 9 October, the Pretender was also proclaimed king in Northumberland. Although they were soon forced to surrender, the English and Scottish rebels, after joining forces at Kelso, entered England on 1 November and occupied Preston. Well off the pace, the Pretender finally landed in Scotland on 22 December. A day later Joseph Addison published the first issue of a new journal, *The Free-Holder.*

The title of Addison's paper is of significance. Following the pattern laid down by William of Orange in 1688, James Stuart tried to pose as the protector of the liberty and property of the British freeholder. Whether or not any but existing Jacobites would have been convinced by the Pretender's rhetoric, Addison's pitch was that, as 'one, who draws his Pen in the Defence of Property', he gloried in the fact that he was 'a *British* Free-Holder'. What the *persona* adopted by Addison actually gloried in was his idealised version of the British constitution. 'A Free-Holder may be either a Voter, or a Knight of the Shire', he explained, 'a Wit, or a Fox-hunter; a Scholar, or a Soldier; an Alderman, or a Courtier; a Patriot, or a Stock-Jobber' (*The Free-Holder* (1716), pp. 1, 2–3).

Despite his protestations, however, Addison's brief was to defend the Protestant succession, blacken the Jacobite rebels, and ridicule those who tacitly supported them. It is not surprising, therefore, that his most memorable papers involved the absurd Fox-hunter, a character who held 'that there had been no good Weather since the Revolution':

> FOR the Honour of His Majesty, and the Safety of His Government, we cannot but observe, that those who have appeared the greatest Enemies to both, are of that

Rank of Men, who are commonly distinguished by the Title of *Fox-hunters*. As several of these have had no Part of their Education in Cities, Camps, or Courts, it is doubtful whether they are of greater Ornament or Use to the Nation in which they live. It would be an everlasting Reproach to Politicks, should such Men be able to overturn an Establishment which has been formed by the wisest Laws, and is supported by the ablest Heads. The wrong Notions and Prejudices which cleave to many of these Countrey-Gentlemen, who have always lived out of the way of being better informed, are not easy to be conceived by a Person who has never conversed with them.

That I may give my Readers an Image of these Rural Statesmen, I shall without farther Preface, set down an Account of a Discourse I chanced to have with one of them some Time ago. I was Travelling towards one of the remote Parts of *England*, when about Three a-Clock in the Afternoon, seeing a Countrey-Gentleman trotting before me with a Spaniel by his Horse's Side, I made up to him. Our Conversation opened, as usual, upon the Weather, in which we were very unanimous, having both agreed that it was too dry for the Season of the Year. My Fellow-Traveller upon this observed to me, that there had been no good Weather since the Revolution. I was a little startled at so extraordinary a Remark, but would not interrupt him till he proceeded to tell me of the fine Weather they used to have in King *Charles* the Second's Reign. I only answered that I did not see how the Badness of the Weather could be the King's Fault; and, without waiting for his Reply, asked him whose House it was we saw upon a Rising-Ground at a little Distance from us. He told me it belonged to an old Fanatical Cur, Mr. Such a one, *You must have heard of him*, says he, *He's one of the Rump.*[6] I knew the Gentleman's Character upon hearing his Name, but assured him that to my Knowledge he was a good Churchman: *Ay!* says he with a kind of Surprize, *We were told in the Countrey, that he spoke twice in the Queen's Time against taking off the Duties upon* French *Claret.* This naturally led us into the Proceedings of late Parliaments, upon which Occasion he affirmed roundly, that there had not been one good Law passed since King *William*'s Accession to the Throne, except the Act for preserving the Game. I had a mind to see him out, and therefore did not care for contradicting him. *Is it not hard, says he, that honest Gentlemen should be taken into Custody of Messengers to prevent them from acting according to their Consciences? But, says he, what can we expect when a Party of Factious Sons of Whores*— He was going on in great Passion, but chanced to miss his Dog, who was amusing himself about a Bush, that grew at some Distance behind us. We stood still till he had whistled him up; when he fell into a long Panegyrick upon his Spaniel, who seem'd indeed excellent in his Kind: But I found the most remarkable Adventure of his Life was, that he had once like to have worried a Dissenting-Teacher. The Master could hardly sit on his Horse for laughing all the while he was giving me the Particulars of this Story, which I found had mightily endeared his Dog to him, and as he himself told me, had made him a great Favourite among all the honest Gentlemen of the Countrey. We were at length diverted from this Piece of Mirth by a Post-Boy, who winding his Horn at us, my Companion gave him two or three Curses, and left the Way clear for him. *I fancy* said *I, that Post brings News from* Scotland. *I shall long to see the next* Gazette. *Sir*, says he, *I make it a Rule never to believe any of your printed News. We never see, Sir, how Things go, except now and then in* Dyer's *Letter, and I read that more for the Style than the News. The Man has a cleaver* Pen it must be own'd. But is it not strange that we *should be making War upon Church of* England *Men, with* Dutch *and* Swiss Soldiers, Men of Antimonarchical Principles? These *Foreigners will never be loved in* England, Sir; they have not *that Wit and Good-breeding that we have.* I must confess I did not expect to hear my new Acquaintance value himself upon these Qualifications, but finding him such a Critick upon Foreigners, I ask'd him if he had ever Travelled; He told me, he did not know what Travelling was good for, but to teach a Man to ride the Great Horse, to jabber *French*, and to talk against Passive-Obedience: To which he added, that he scarce ever knew a Traveller in his Life

who had not forsook his Principles, and lost his Hunt-
ing-Seat. *For my Part*, says he, *I and my Father before me
have always been for Passive-Obedience, and shall be always for
opposing a Prince who makes use of Ministers that are of another
Opinion.*

Joseph Addison, *The Free-Holder, Or Political
Essays* (1716), pp. 121–4

Addison's Fox-hunter served to caricature the oath-swearing,
crypto-Jacobite country gentleman. He was a freeholder, to be
sure, but the wrong sort of freeholder. It is curious to find a
Whig like Addison, an adherent of Revolution principles, nevertheless preaching that 'Rebellion is one of the most hainous
Crimes which it is in the Power of Man to commit' (*The
Free-Holder*, p. 70), but this was only one of the ideological
tangles into which the Whigs were drawn after the Hanoverian
succession. If the Tories had had difficulty reconciling their
beliefs with the events of 1688, the Whigs experienced problems
of their own after 1714.

Even though the rebellion was effectively over (the Pretender
fled from Scotland on 4 February), *habeas corpus* was suspended
for a further six-month period on 21 January 1716. The ending
of the practice of imprisonment without trial had been one of
the achievements of the first Whigs. Now their successors were
its advocates. It might be argued that this was merely an
emergency measure, but the same justification could scarcely be
given for the passing of the Septennial Act. The Triennial Act,
which called for new Parliamentary elections every three years,
had been one of the key Whig achievements of the Revolution
Settlement. The arguments put forward in favour of triennial
parliaments – that they would help to prevent Court interference
with parliamentary proceedings – were no less powerful in 1716
than they had been in 1694. Hidden beneath concern for the
security of the Protestant succession, the Septennial Act was a
flagrant attempt to perpetuate Whig power. Not even the Act of
Settlement was sacrosanct, as the clause restricting the King's
movement abroad became the latest of the limitations in the
original statute to disappear.

Such changes in Whig attitudes did not pass without comment.
Political ideologies modify over time like everything else, but

those who had been accustomed to regard Whiggery as basically a principle of independence from, if not opposition to, the Court found it particularly hard to contemplate a Whig government which openly flouted 'Old Whig' tenets. In the appropriately titled *Cato's Letters* John Trenchard and Thomas Gordon criticised the threat posed to liberty by the conduct of these 'new' Whigs in much the same style as Trenchard, over twenty years previously, had attacked William III's ministers over their attitude to standing armies:

> *SIR,*
>
> THE *English* Climate, famous for variable Weather, is not less famous for variable Parties, which fall insensibly into an Exchange of Principles, and yet go on to hate and curse one another for these Principles. A *Tory* under Oppression, or out of a Place, is a *Whig*; and a *Whig* with Power to oppress, is a *Tory*. The *Tory* damns the *Whig* for maintaining a Resistance, which he himself never fails to practise; and the *Whig* reproaches the *Tory* with slavish Principles, and yet calls him Rebel if he does not practise them. The Truth is, all Men dread the Power of Oppression out of their own Hands, and almost all Men wish it irresistible when it is there.
>
> We change Sides every Day, yet keep the same Names for ever. I have known a Man a staunch *Whig* for a Year together, yet thought and called a *Tory* by all the *Whigs*, and by the *Tories* themselves. I have known him afterwards fall in with the *Whigs*, and act another Year like a *Tory*, that is, do blindly what he was bid, and serve the Interest of Power, right or wrong: And then all the *Tories* have agreed to call him a *Whig*; whereas all the while he was called a *Tory*, he was a *Whig*, and afterwards by joining with the *Whigs*, he became an Apostate from *Whiggism*, and turned *Tory*.
>
> So wildly do Men run on to confound Names and Things: We call Men opprobriously *Tories*, for practising the best Part of *Whiggism*; and honourably christen our selves *Whigs*, when we are openly acting the vilest parts of *Toryism*, such Parts as the *Tories* never attempted to act.
>
> To know fully the Signification of Words, we must go

to their Source. The Original Principle of a *Tory*, was to let the Crown do what it pleased; yet no People opposed and restrained the Crown more, when they themselves did not serve and direct the Crown. The Original Principle of a *Whig*, was to be no further for the Interest of the Crown, than the Crown was for the Interest of the People. – A Principle founded upon everlasting Reason, and which the *Tories* have come into as often as Temptations were taken out of their Way; and a Principle which the *Whigs*, whenever they have had Temptations, have as vilely renounced in Practice. No Men upon Earth have been more servile, crouching, and abandoned Creatures of Power, than the *Whigs* sometimes have been; I mean some former *Whigs*.

The *Tories* therefore are often *Whigs* without knowing it; and the *Whigs* are *Tories* without owning it. To prove this, it is enough to reflect upon Times and Instances, when the asserting of Liberty, the legal and undoubted Liberties of *England*, has been called *Libelling* by those professed Patrons of Liberty, the *Whigs*; and they have taken extravagant, arbitrary, and violent Methods, to suppress the very Sound of it; whilst the *Tories* have maintained and defended it, and put Checks upon those, who, tho' they had risen by its Name, were eager to suppress its Spirit, and had appointed for that worthy End an Inquisition, new to the Constitution, and threatening its Overthrow: An Inquisition, where Men were used as Criminals without a Crime, and charged with Crimes without a Name, and treated in some Respects, as if they had been guilty of the highest.

> John Trenchard and Thomas Gordon,
> *Cato's Letters* (1724), III, 206–8

Additional impetus for the close scrutiny of the moral basis of Whig ideology in the early 1720s was supplied by the scandal of the South Sea Bubble. Indeed, the reason *Cato's Letters* began appearing in *The London Journal* in November 1720 was 'to call for publick justice upon the wicked Managers of the [. . .] *South-Sea* Scheme'. Although it is usual to think of the controlling metaphor of the Bubble as some sort of hot-air balloon, in contemporary parlance it was rather more serious than that. Quite simply, to '*bubble*' someone was to cheat or deceive them, and *a* 'bubble' was either the victim of a confidence-trick or the actual 'con' itself. The South Sea Bubble then was a massive 'con' which raised troubling questions about public and private morality. It was, in short, an enormous crisis of confidence in the system of public credit, which had itself been the cause of major social repercussions in the years following the Revolution.

In 1720, the Directors of the South Sea Company quite cynically manipulated the market value of its stock so that it soared. Investors were encouraged to buy at a highly inflated price. When the crash came and fortunes were lost, there was a public outcry. In one of his most frequently reprinted poems, Swift openly accused the South Sea Directors of fraud:

> *Directors!* for 'tis you I warn,
> By long Experience we have found
>   What Planet rul'd when you were born;
> We see you never can be drown'd;
>
>   Beware, nor over-bulky grow,
> Nor come within your Cully's Reach;
>   For if the Sea should sink so low,
> To leave you dry upon the Beach;
>
>   You'll owe your Ruin to your Bulk;
> Your Foes already waiting stand,
>   To tear you like a founder'd Hulk,
> While you lie helpless on the Sand.
>
>   Thus when a Whale has lost the Tide,
> The Coasters crowd to seize the Spoil;
>   The Monster into Parts divide,
> And strip the Bones, and melt the Oil.
>
>   Oh! may some *Western* Tempest sweep
> These *Locusts*, whom our Fruits have fed,
>   That Plague, *Directors*, to the Deep,
> Driven from the *South-Sea* to the *Red*.
>
>   May He, whom Nature's Laws obey,
> Who *lifts* the Poor, and *sinks* the Proud,

Quiet the raging of the Sea,
And *still the Madness of the Croud.*

But never shall our Isle have Rest,
Till those devouring *Swine* run down,
    (*The Devil's leaving the Possest*)
And *headlong in the Waters drown.*

The Nation too too late will find,
Computing all their Cost and Trouble,
    Directors Promises but Wind,
South-Sea at best a mighty *Bubble.*

Jonathan Swift, *The Bubble* (1721), pp. 5–6, 19, 21–3

Embezzlement on such a large scale was something new in the
early eighteenth century, and the South Sea Bubble seemed to
contemporaries to threaten the very social structure. Trenchard
and Gordon put it this way:

> Whether the Directors and their Masters shall be pun-
> ish'd or no, is to me one and the same Question, as to
> ask, whether you will preserve your Constitution or no,
> or whether you will have any Constitution at all? It is a
> Contention of Honesty and Innocence with Villainy and
> Falshood; it is a Dispute whether or no you shall be a
> People; it is a Struggle, and, if it is baulk'd, will, in all
> probability, be the last Struggle for old *English* Liberty.
> All this is well understood by the People of *England.*

John Trenchard and Thomas Gordon,
Cato's Letters (1724), I, 160

It was suspected (with reason) that the buck stopped very high
up indeed and that members of the royal family were implicated
in the dealings of the South Sea Company. As a consequence,
there was a good, old-fashioned cover-up and it was left to
satirists like Swift to vent their outrage in print. It is in the light
of the South Sea Bubble that the following passage about
Lilliputian customs should be read:

THEY look upon Fraud as a greater Crime than Theft,

and therefore seldom fail to punish it with Death; for they alledge, that Care and Vigilance, with a very common Understanding, may preserve a Man's Goods from Thieves, but Honesty has no fence against superior Cunning: and since it is necessary that there should be a perpetual Intercourse of Buying and Selling, and dealing upon Credit, where Fraud is permitted or connived at, or hath no Law to punish it, the honest Dealer is always undone, and the Knave gets the advantage. I remember when I was once interceeding with the King for a Criminal who had wronged his Master of a great Sum of Money, which he had received by Order, and ran away with; and happening to tell his Majesty, by way of Extenuation, that it was only a Breach of Trust; The Emperor thought it monstrous in me to offer, as a Defence, the greatest Aggravation of the Crime: and truly I had little to say in return, farther than the common Answer, that different Nations had different Customs; for, I confess, I was heartily ashamed.

Jonathan Swift, *Gulliver's Travels* (1726) Part I, pp. 95–6

As a response to the new Whig ideology Swift, like Trenchard, resorted to the traditional paternalistic ideal espoused and propounded by the pantheon of 'Old Whig' or 'Commonwealth' writers – Algernon Sidney, John Locke, Robert Molesworth, 'and other Dangerous Authors, who talk of *Liberty as a Blessing, to which the whole Race of Mankind hath an original Title, whereof nothing but unlawful Force can divest them*' (Swift, *A Letter to the Right Honourable the Lord Viscount Molesworth* (1724), p. 9). It must be stressed that, as we have seen, although these 'Dangerous Authors' were radical Whig ideologues, their radicalism, like Swift's, was of a conservative nature.

To demonstrate the truth of this, two final passages from Swift must suffice. For 'Old Whig' ideology to work, the hierarchical nature of society had to be strictly maintained, and Swift duly preached on the text of 'the poor man's contentment with his lot'. But what if those in positions of authority failed to look after their dependents? What, in short, would happen if the paternalistic system broke down, as seemed to be happening in Ireland?

> I have heard *Great* Divines affirm, that *nothing is so likely to call down an universal judgment from Heaven upon a Nation as universal Oppression*; and whether this be not already verified in part, *their Worships* the Landlords are *now* at full leisure to consider. Whoever Travels this Country, and observes the *Face* of Nature, or the *Faces*, and Habits, and Dwellings of the *Natives*, will hardly think himself in a Land where either *Law*, *Religion*, or *common Humanity* is professed.
>
> Jonathan Swift, *A Proposal For the universal Use of Irish Manufacture* (1721), pp. 14–15

In these circumstances the ideological underpinning of society was perceived to be in danger of giving way. Something was necessary to prop it up and, of course, the staunchest support of all was religion:

> I SHALL now say something about that great number of poor, who, under the name of common beggars, infest our streets, and fill our Ears with their continual Cries, and craving Importunity. This I shall venture to call an unnecessary Evil, brought upon us for the gross Neglect, and want of proper Management, in those whose Duty it is to prevent it: But, before I proceed farther, let me humbly presume to vindicate the Justice and Mercy of God and his Dealings with Mankind. Upon this Particular He hath not dealt so hardly with his Creatures as some would imagine, when they see so many miserable Objects ready to perish for Want: For it would infallibly be found, upon strict Enquiry, that there is hardly one in twenty of those miserable Objects who do not owe their present Poverty to their own Faults; to their present Sloth and Negligence; to their indiscreet Marriage without the least Prospect of supporting a Family, to their foolish Expensiveness, to their Drunkenness, and other Vices, by which they have squandered their Gettings, and contracted Diseases in their old Age. And, to speak freely, is it any Way reasonable or just, that those who have denied themselves many lawful Satisfactions, and Conveniences of Life, from a Principle of

Conscience, as well as Prudence, that they might not be a Burthen to the Public, should be charged with support-ing Others, who have brought themselves to less than a morsel of Bread by their Idleness, Extravagance, and Vice? Yet such and no other, are for the greatest Number not only in those who beg in our Streets, but even of what we call poor decayed House-keepers, whom we are apt to pity as real Objects of Charity, and distinguish them from common Beggars [. . . .]

Jonathan Swift, 'Causes of the Wretched Condition of Ireland', *Works* (1772), IX, 62–3

While Swift, like Trenchard and Gordon, posed disconcerting questions about apparent changes in Whig ideology and linked them to wider questions about the foundations of eighteenth-century society, Bernard Mandeville's original and disturbing analysis of human motivation formed the basis of a much more radical critique. *The Fable of the Bees: Or, Private Vices, Publick Benefits* was written, according to Mandeville,

to shew the Impossibility of enjoying all the most elegant Comforts of Life that are to be met with in an indus-trious, wealthy and powerful Nation, and at the same time be bless'd with all the Virtue and Innocence that can be wish'd for in a Golden Age; from thence to expose the Unreasonableness and Folly of those, that desirous of being an opulent and flourishing People, and wonderfully greedy after all the Benefits they can receive as such, are yet always murmuring at and exclaiming against those Vices and Inconveniences, that from the Beginning of the World to this present Day, have been inseparable from all the Kingdoms and States that ever were fam'd for Strength, Riches, and Politeness at the same time.

Bernard Mandeville, *The Fable of the Bees: Or, Private Vices, Publick Benefits* (1724), Preface

The novel proposition that economic strength was inextricably linked to vice and corruption was not one which was likely to be generally accepted. It smacked too much of the dangerous, new ideas of Hobbes. But Mandeville claimed

> to have demonstrated that, neither the Friendly Qualities and kind Affections that are natural to Man, nor the real Virtues he is capable of acquiring by Reason and Self-Denial, are the Foundation of Society; but that what we call Evil in this World, Moral as well as Natural, is the grand Principle that makes us sociable Creatures, the solid Basis, the Life and Support of all Trades and Employments without Exception: That there we must look for the true Origin of all Arts and Sciences, and that the Moment Evil ceases, the Society must be spoiled, if not totally dissolved.
>
> Bernard Mandeville, *The Fable of the Bees: Or, Private Vices, Publick Benefits* (1724), pp. 427–8

Mandeville left the reader cogitating uncomfortably on 'the seeming Paradox, the Substance of which is advanc'd in the Title Page; that Private Vices by the dextrous Management of a skilful Politician may be turn'd into Publick Benefits'.

The world of Defoe's *Moll Flanders* is sometimes viewed as Hobbesian and a reaction to post-Revolution moral confusion. This may well be true, but perhaps it is at least as much a fictional working-out of Mandeville's ideas. This is how the narrative proper begins:

> I HAVE been told, that in one of our Neighbour Nations, whether it be in *France*, or where else, I know not; they have an Order from the King, that when any Criminal is condemn'd, either to Die, or to the Gallies, or to be Transported, if they leave any Children, as such are generally unprovided for, by the Poverty or Forfeiture of their Parents; so they are immediately taken into the Care of the Government, and put into an Hospital call'd the *House* of *Orphans*, where they are Bred up, Cloath'd, Fed, Taught, and when fit to go out, are plac'd out to Trades, or to Services, so as to be well able to provide for themselves by an honest industrious Behaviour.
>
> HAD this been the Custom in our Country, I had not

been left a poor desolate Girl without Friends, without Cloaths, without Help or Helper in the World, as was my Fate; and by which, I was not only expos'd to very great Distresses, even before I was capable, either of Understanding my Case, or how to Amend it, nor brought into a Course of Life, which was not only scandalous in itself, but, which in its ordinary Course, tended to the swift Destruction both of Soul and Body.

BUT the Case was otherwise here, my Mother was convicted of Felony for a certain petty Theft, scarce worth naming, (*viz.*) Having an opportunity of borrowing three Pieces of fine *Holland*, of a certain Draper in *Cheapside*: The Circumstances are too long to repeat, and I have heard them related so many Ways, that I can scarce be certain, which is the right Account.

HOWEVER it was, this they all agree in, that my Mother pleaded her Belly, and being found quick with Child she was respited for about seven Months, in which time having brought me into the World, and being about again, she was call'd Down, as they term it, to her former Judgment, but obtain'd the Favour of being Transported to the Plantations, and left me about Half a Year old; and in bad Hands you may be sure.

THIS is too near the first Hours of my Life, for me to relate any thing of myself, but by hear say, 'tis enough to mention, that as I was born in such an unhappy Place, I had no Parish to have Recourse to for my Nourishment in my Infancy, nor can I give the least Account how I was kept alive; other, than that as I have been told, some Relation of my Mothers took me away for a while as a Nurse, but at whose Expence, or by whose Direction I know nothing at all of it.

Daniel Defoe, *Moll Flanders* (1722), pp. 2–3

What is most interesting about the opening paragraphs of Defoe's fictional autobiography is the way in which the narrator first gestures in the direction of a particular social reform, as if anticipating the future 'novel of social protest', before turning to the vilification of those responsible for her later plight. At the same time the verbal register abruptly alters to reveal the older

Moll Flanders who, as the Preface explains, writes 'in language more like one still in *Newgate* than one grown penitent and humble, as she afterwards pretends to be'. Thus her mother's felony – 'a certain petty Theft, scarce worth naming' – is called 'Having an opportunity of borrowing three Pieces of fine *Holland*, of a certain Draper in *Cheapside*', before Moll goes on to explain how she 'pleaded her Belly' in order to escape the gallows.

Numerous examples within the narrative bear witness to the eponymous anti-heroine's flagrant attempts to shift the responsibilities for her own moral decisions on to others. Moll steals a necklace of gold beads from 'a pretty little Child [which] had been at a Dancing-School, and was going home, all alone'. She admits that 'the Devil put me upon killing the Child in the dark Alley, that it might not Cry', but thinks better of it. Because of these 'tender Thoughts', Moll decides to place the blame for her crime elsewhere:

> as I did the poor Child no harm, I only said to my self, I had given the Parents a just Reproof for their Negligence in leaving the poor little Lamb to come home by it self, and it would teach them to take more Care of it another time.
>
> THIS String of Beads was worth about Twelve or Fourteen Pounds, I suppose it might have been formerly the Mother's, for it was too big for the Child's wear, but that, perhaps, the Vanity of the Mother to have her Child look Fine at the Dancing School, had made her let the Child wear it, and no doubt the Child had a Maid sent to take care of it, but she, like a careless Jade, was taken up perhaps with some Fellow that had met her by the way, and so the poor Baby wandred till it fell into my Hands.
>
> Daniel Defoe, *Moll Flanders* (1722), p. 238

By spinning an elaborate fiction involving the child's mother, the maid which (doubtless) had been sent to accompany the child, and 'some Fellow' she had (apparently) met, Moll successfully distances herself from what she has done, unloading her moral responsibilities in the process. This is not the only time she does this. Later on in her story, for instance, she rolls a drunk, who has been so imprudent as to invite her into his coach, with all the practised ease of the *habitué* of the criminal world which she has become. Rather than apologising to the reader for her actions, however, Moll draws from them a moral which, for its audacity, is little short of breath-taking.

> WOULD such Gentlemen but consider the contempt-ible Thoughts which the very Women they are concern'd with, in such Cases as these, have of them, it wou'd be a surfeit to them [. . .] I CAME home with this last Booty to my Governess, and really when I told her the Story it so affected her, that she was hardly able to forbear Tears, to think how such a Gentleman run a daily Risque of being undone, every time a Glass of Wine got into his Head.
>
> BUT as to the Purchase I got, and how entirely I stript him, she told me it pleas'd her wonderfully; nay, Child, *says she*, the usage may, for ought I know, do more to reform him, than all the Sermons that ever he will hear in his Life, and if the remainder of the Story be true, so it did.
>
> Daniel Defoe, *Moll Flanders* (1722), pp. 279–80

It is unnecessary to claim that Defoe in *Moll Flanders* was somehow projecting Mandeville's new morality on to the society in which he lived, but there is undoubtedly a fortuitous coin-cidence between the date of publication of Defoe's narrative, and the stir occasioned by the third edition of *The Fable of the Bees*, which was presented by the Grand Jury of Middlesex in 1723.

No nine days' wonder, Mandeville's notoriety was sufficiently disturbing for Fielding to take up the cudgels against his scandalous ideas not only in a number of his other works, but in the opening chapter of Book VI of *Tom Jones*, where once again Mandeville is implicitly linked with that other author of 'noxious and combustible doctrines', Thomas Hobbes:

> IN our last Book we have been obliged to deal pretty much with the Passion of Love; and, in our succeeding Book, shall be forced to handle this Subject still more

largely. It may not, therefore, in this Place, be improper to apply ourselves to the Examination of that modern Doctrine, by which certain Philosophers, among many other wonderful discoveries, pretend to have found out, that there is no such Passion in the human Breast.

Whether these Philosophers be the same with that surprizing Sect, who are honourably mentioned by the late Dr. *Swift*, as having, by the mere Force of Genius alone, without the least Assistance of any Kind of Learning, or even Reading, discovered that profound and invaluable Secret, That there was no G[od] or whether they are not rather the same with those who, some Years since, very much alarmed the World, by shewing that there were no such things as Virtue or Goodness really existing in Human Nature, and who deduced our best Actions from Pride, I will not here presume to determine [. . .] To avoid, however, all Contention, if possible, with these Philosophers, if they will be called so; and to shew our own Disposition to accommodate Matters peaceably between us, we shall here make them some Concessions, which may possibly put an End to the dispute [. . .] In return to all these Concessions, I desire of the Philosophers to grant, that there is in some (I believe in many) human Breasts, a kind and benevolent Disposition, which is gratified by contributing to the Happiness of others. That in this Gratification alone, as in Friendship, in parental and filial Affection, and indeed in general Philanthropy, there is a great and exquisite Delight. That if we will not call such Disposition Love, we have no Name for it. That though the Pleasures arising from such pure Love may be heightened and sweetened by the Assistance of amorous Desires, yet the former can subsist alone, nor are they destroyed by the Intervention of the latter. Lastly, That Esteem and Gratitude are the proper Motives to Love, as Youth and Beauty are to Desire; and therefore though such Desire may naturally cease, when Age or Sickness overtake its Object, yet these can have no Effect on Love, nor ever shake or remove from a good Mind, that Sensation or Passion which hath Gratitude and Esteem for its Basis.

To deny the Existence of a Passion of which we often
see manifest Instances, seems ·to be very strange and
absurd [. . . .]

Henry Fielding, Tom Jones (1749), II, 222–6

Fielding's novel is clearly informed by the contemporary debate
on human nature which, working through a carefully constructed
series of binary oppositions, attempts to force the reader. to
confront a number of uncomfortable propositions about human
behaviour. The most obvious of these comparisons is that
between Tom Jones and his half-brother, Blifil:

> As there are some Minds whose Affections, like
> Master *Blifil*'s, are solely placed on one single Person,
> whose Interest and indulgence alone they consider on
> every Occasion; regarding the Good and Ill of all others
> as merely indifferent, any farther than as they contribute
> to the Pleasure or Advantage of that Person: So there is
> a different Temper of mind which borrows a Degree of
> Virtue even from Self-love; such can never receive any
> kind of Satisfaction from another, without loving the
> Creature to whom that Satisfaction is owing, and with-
> out making its Well-being in some sort necessary to their
> own Ease.
> Of this latter Species was our Heroe [. . . .]

Henry Fielding, Tom Jones (1749), II, 45

In Fielding's hands the rational egoist of Hobbes' *Leviathan*,
and Mandeville's insistence that vice, rather than virtue, con-
stitutes the bonds of which society is comprised, are subtly
melded together in the creation of the character of the
utterly self-interested Blifil. Tom's character, on the other hand,
appears to reflect the optimistic concept of human nature
portrayed in Anthony Ashley Cooper, the third Earl of Shaftesbury, in his book, *Characteristicks of Men, Manners, Opinions, Times*
(1711).

Shaftesbury insisted that men were naturally virtuous, and that
vice was a perversion of human nature, just as Tom, in his
dialogue with the Man of the Hill, maintains that 'Nothing

should be esteemed as characteristical of a Species, but what is to be found among the best and most perfect Individuals of that Species'. Mandeville himself drew attention to the differences between his beliefs and Shaftesbury's, making it very clear that, because it was misleading, Shaftesbury's was the kind of naïve optimism which he discounted:

> THE Generality of Moralists and Philosophers have hitherto agreed that there could be no Virtue without Self-denial; but a late Author, who is now much read by Men of Sense, is of a contrary Opinion, and imagines that Men without any Trouble or Violence upon themselves may be naturally Virtuous. He seems to require and expects Goodness in his Species, as we do a sweet Taste in Grapes and China Oranges, of which, if any of them are sour, we boldly pronounce that they are not come to that Perfection their Nature is capable of. This Noble Writer (for it is the Lord *Shaft[e]sbury* I mean in his Characteristicks) Fancies, that as Man is made for Society, so he ought to be born with a kind Affection to the whole, of which he is a part, and a Propensity to seek the Welfare of it. In pursuance of this Supposition, he calls every Action perform'd with regard to the Publick Good, Virtuous; and all Selfishness, wholly excluding such a Regard, Vice. In respect to our Species he looks upon Virtue and Vice as permanent Realities that must ever be the same in all Countries and all Ages, and imagines that a Man of sound Understanding, by following the rules of good Sense, may not only find out that *Pulchrum & Honestum* both in Morality and the Works of Art and Nature, but likewise govern himself by his Reason with as much Ease and Readiness as a good Rider manages a well taught Horse by the Bridle.
>
> The attentive Reader, who perused the foregoing part of this Book, will soon perceive that two Systems cannot be more opposite than his Lordship's and mine. His Notions I confess are generous and refined: They are a high Compliment to Human-kind, and capable by the help of a little Enthusiasm of Inspiring us with the most Noble Sentiments concerning the Dignity

of our exalted Nature: What pity it is that they are not true!

Bernard Mandeville, *The Fable of the Bees: Or, Private Vices, Publick Benefits* (1724), pp. 371–3

In effect, Mandeville was interrogating the ideology behind Shaftesbury's analysis of human nature. If, as Mandeville maintained, progress was possible only as a result of the economic stimulus supplied by private vices, then what was behind Shaftesbury's insistence that 'virtue' was the cement bonding society together? The unpalatable conclusion would seem to be that Shaftesbury was trying to provide an alternative justification for the existing social structure, with 'virtue' replacing religion as its central supporting pillar.

Mandeville's was an uncomfortable doctrine which appeared to threaten the moral and religious bases of not only British, but European society. Its political implications were far-reaching. Mandeville's paradoxes provided additional stimulus to the ideological questionings which had been prompted by the South Sea Bubble, and which, in turn, had been complicated by the political changes resulting from the Hanoverian succession. Many previously unexamined beliefs were in the process of being reassessed, and defenders of the traditional concept of a hierarchical society based on benevolent paternalism were at pains to refute the dangerous, new ideas which were being aired in print. It is difficult to say with any certainty how much Fielding's ideas were influenced by Pope as well as Shaftesbury, but it was in the *Essay on Man* that the most famous connection between virtue and self-love was made, as Pope sought to analyse 'Th'according music of a well-mix'd State':

Such is the World's great harmony, that springs
From Order, Union, full Consent of things!
Where small and great, where weak and mighty, made
To serve, not suffer, strengthen, not invade,
More pow'rful each as needful to the rest,
And, in proportion as it blesses, blest,
Draw to one point, and to one centre bring
Beast, Man, or Angel, Servant, Lord, or King.

> For Forms of Government let fools contest;
> Whate'er is best administer'd is best:
> For Modes of Faith, let graceless zealots fight;
> His can't be wrong whose life is in the right:
> In Faith and Hope the world will disagree,
> But all Mankind's concern is Charity:
> All must be false that thwart this One great End,
> And all of God, that bless Mankind or mend.
> Man, like the gen'rous vine, supported lives;
> The strength he gains is from th'embrace he gives.
> On their own Axis as the Planets run,
> Yet make at once their circle round the Sun:
> So two consistent motions act the Soul;
> And one regards Itself, and one the Whole.
> Thus God and Nature link'd the gen'ral frame,
> And bade Self-love and Social be the same.

Alexander Pope, *An Essay on Man* (1743), pp. 75–9

However, the awesome complacency of Pope's doctrine – 'Whatever IS, is RIGHT' – was perhaps less important as an attempt to shore up a tottering providential ideology than as the philosophical foundation of the platform which was hastily being constructed to confront the more immediate political threat of Robert Walpole.

5   The Opposition to Walpole

THROUGH all the Employments of Life
Each Neighbour abuses his Brother;
Whore and Rogue, they call Husband and Wife:
All Professions be-rogue one another.
The Priest calls the Lawyer a cheat,
The Lawyer be-knaves the Divine;
And the Statesman, because he's so great,
Thinks his Trade as honest as mine.

John Gay, *The Beggar's Opera* (1728), p. 1

Public and private morality were now under the microscope, and in the person of Sir Robert Walpole, the first or 'prime' minister of George I, the age was provided with a massive example to praise or to censure. As he was an obvious target, the 'Great Man' quickly became for Augustan satirists the type of the unscrupulous, self-seeking politician. His contemporary reputation had not benefited from his involvement in both the South Sea Bubble cover-up (as a consequence of which he earned himself the nick-name of the 'Skreenmaster-General') and the impeachment in 1723 of Francis Atterbury, Bishop of Rochester, for Jacobite plotting. Walpole's exploitation of the latter, 'the most successful political scare in the eighteenth century' (G.V. Bennett, 'Jacobitism and the rise of Walpole', *Historical Perspectives* (1974), p. 71), ensured that the safety of the Protestant succession would remain high on the political agenda, and that all opposition activity was liable to be smeared with the charge of Jacobitism by ministerial propagandists.

By the middle of the 1720s the battle-lines were drawn, and an extraordinary assault was launched by the most gifted writers of the early eighteenth century not only on Walpole's own probity, but on the integrity of the Hanoverian regime itself. The works of Swift, Pope, Gay, Thomson, Fielding and the young Samuel Johnson are shot through with references to Walpole and to the alleged corruption of his administration, as the Scriblerian satirists and their allies sought to draw attention to what they perceived as the nation's overwhelming moral degeneracy. What they were actually complaining about was the threat being posed to the old paternalistic ways by upstarts like Walpole, who were seemingly untroubled by the possible effects of neglecting the welfare of 'the lower sort of people'. However, as we shall see, this ideological concern for a particular social perspective readily tipped over into an expression of anxiety for the condition of religion and morality under the Hanoverians.

Swift fired the opening salvo in *Gulliver's Travels*, in which there are unmistakable allusions to Walpole in the character of Flimnap, the Lilliputian Treasurer, who 'is allowed to cut a Caper on the strait Rope, at least an Inch higher than any other Lord in the whole Empire', and to the Atterbury affair in the discussion of methods 'for discovering Plots and Conspiracies against the Government' in Part III (*Travels into Several Remote Nations of the World* (1726), Part I, p. 49; Part III, pp. 88–9). Swift's most scathing criticism of the system of Walpole also works indirectly, through implication rather than direct statement. It occurs during Gulliver's account of his long conversations with the King of Brobdingnag, in the course of which Swift manages to touch upon most of the key points of ideology at issue between Walpole and the opposition.

Gulliver offers an encomium on his 'own dear native Country':

> I BEGAN my Discourse by informing his Majesty that our Dominions consisted of two Islands, which composed three mighty Kingdoms under one Sovereign, besides our Plantations in *America*. I dwelt long upon the Fertility of our Soil, and the Temperature of our Climate. I then spoke at large upon the Constitution of an *English* Parliament, partly made up of an illustrious Body called the House of Peers, Persons of the noblest Blood, and of the most ancient and ample Patrimonies. I described that extraordinary Care always taken of their Education in Arts and Arms, to qualify them for being Counsellors born to the King and Kingdom, to have a Share in the Legislature, to be Members of the highest Court of Judicature from whence there could be no Appeal; and to be Champions always ready for the Defence of their Prince and Country by their Valour, Conduct and Fi-

delity. That these were the Ornament and Bulwark of the Kingdom, worthy Followers of their most renowned Ancestors, whose Honor had been the Reward of their Virtue, from which their Posterity were never once known to degenerate. To these were joined several holy Persons, as part of that Assembly, under the Title of Bishops; whose peculiar Business it is, to take care of Religion, and of those who instruct the People therein. These were searched and sought out through the whole Nation, by the Prince and his wisest Counsellors, among such of the Priesthood, as were most deservedly distinguished by the Sanctity of their Lives, and the Depth of their Erudition; who were indeed the spiritual Fathers of the Clergy and the People.

THAT, the other Part of the Parliament consisted as an Assembly called the House of Commons; who were all principal Gentlemen, *freely* picked and culled out by the People themselves, for their great Abilities, and Love of their Country, to represent the Wisdom of the whole Nation. And, these two Bodies make up the most august Assembly in *Europe*, to whom, in Conjunction with the Prince, the whole Legislature is committed.

Jonathan Swift, *Gulliver's Travels* (1726), Part I, pp. 108–10

Earlier in his narrative, in describing the laws and customs of the Lilliputians, Gulliver explained how he 'would only be understood to mean the original Institutions, and not the most scandalous Corruptions into which these People are fallen by the degenerate Nature of Man' (Part I, pp. 99–100). Quite clearly, the same might be said about his description of the British political system. For greater satiric effect Gulliver is made by Swift innocently to represent the 'ancient constitution' to the King of Brobdingnag in all its pristine purity, a condition from which it has long since degenerated. This is made absolutely apparent as soon as the King questions Gulliver about his account:

WHEN I had put an End to these long Discourses, his Majesty in a sixth Audience consulting his Notes, proposed many Doubts, Queries, and Objections, upon every Article. He asked, what Methods were used to cultivate the Minds and Bodies of our young Nobility, and in what kind of Business they commonly spent the first and teachable Part of their Lives. What Course was taken to supply that Assembly when any noble Family became extinct. What Qualifications were necessary in those who are to be created new Lords: Whether the Humour of the Prince, a Sum of Money to a Court-Lady, or a Prime Minister, or a Design of strengthning a Party opposite to the publick Interest, ever happened to be Motives in those Advancements. What Share of Knowledge these Lords had in the Laws of their Country, and how they came by it, so as to enable them to decide the Properties of their Fellow-Subjects in the last Resort. Whether they were always so free from Avarice, Partialities, or Want, that a Bribe, or some other sinister View, could have no Place among them. Whether those holy Lords I spoke of were always promoted to that Rank upon Account of their Knowledge in religious Matters, and the Sanctity of their Lives, had never been Compliers with the times while they were common Priests, or slavish prostitute Chaplains to some Nobleman, whose Opinions they continued servilely to follow after they were admitted into that Assembly.

He then desired to know what Arts were practised in electing those whom I called Commoners. Whether, a Stranger with a strong Purse might not influence the vulgar Voters to chuse him before their own Landlord, or the most considerable Gentleman in the Neighbourhood. How it came to pass, that People were so violently bent upon getting into this Assembly, which I allowed to be a great Trouble and Expence, often to the Ruin of their Families, without any Salary or Pension: Because this appeared such an exalted strain of Virtue and publick Spirit, that his Majesty seemed to doubt it might possibly not be always sincere: And he desired to know whether such zealous Gentlemen could have any Views of refunding themselves for the Charges and Trouble they were at, by sacrificing the Publick Good to the Designs of a weak and vicious Prince in Conjunction with a corrupted Ministry. He multiplied his Questions, and sifted me thoroughly upon every Part of this Head, proposing numberless Enquiries and Objections, which I think it not prudent or convenient to repeat.

Jonathan Swift, *Gulliver's Travels* (1726), Part II, pp. 111–12

The King of Brobdingnag's probing questions dispel the illusion that all is well in Britain under the governance of Walpole, as Swift gives us a perfect illustration of the satirical technique of contrasting things *as they are*, with things *as they should be*. This discrepancy is carefully brought into prominence while Gulliver is under interrogation: Swift even makes Gulliver admit that he did his best to hide 'the Frailties and Deformities of [his] Political Mother', boasting that he 'artfully eluded many of [the King's] Questions, and gave to every Point a more favourable turn by many Degrees than the strictness of Truth would allow' (*Gulliver's Travels*, Part II, p. 123).

In conclusion, 'the Judicious Reader' of *Gulliver's Travels* is reminded of 'the *Brobdingnagians*, whose wise Maxims in Morality and Government, it would be our Happiness to observe' (*Gulliver's Travels*, Part IV, p. 188). The vital connection made by Swift between a nation's manners and its political institutions is central to the ideological point he is trying to get across. In contrast to Britain's current leaders, the King of Brobdingnag, a stern paternalist who is 'almost adored by his Subjects', is a true moral leader of his people. By implication, George I and Walpole, his prime minister, are found wanting when measured against a yardstick such as this.

It did not take very long for judicious readers to discern 'that, under the Allegory of a Voyager, Mr. Gulliver gives us an admirable System of modern Politicks' (*A Key, Being Observations and Explanatory Notes, upon the Travels of Lemuel Gulliver* (1726), p. 5). What was to become the pre-eminent opposition journal, *The Craftsman, or, the Countryman's Journal*, was launched on 1 December 1726 in the immediate aftermath of the publication of *Gulliver's Travels*. It also tried to make political capital out of Swift's assault on the system of Walpole. As the following passage from an early issue suggests, the Great Man was *The Craftsman*'s perennial target:

THERE is nothing, in which the generality of mankind

are so apt to be mistaken, as in their opinion of *Great Men*. They commonly judge by the outside; and where they see power, riches, and splendor, they hastily conclude, that there must be great parts and abilities in proportion: as for Honesty, it is quite out of the question; for even the vulgar herd know better than always to look for that qualification in a modern *Great Man*. But most persons, who have not been much conversant in publick affairs, entertain a better opinion of their Superiors than they generally deserve. They imagine them, at least, to be men of extraordinary capacities, whatever their moral principles may be [. . . .]

The Craftsman (1728), pp. 70–1

This was a development of some significance in the growing campaign to discredit Walpole: the opposition sought to represent him not only as dishonest and irredeemably immoral – the implication was that such things went without saying – but as a man of only meagre abilities regardless of his exalted political position.

Despite the best efforts of the opposition writers, Walpole nevertheless clung on to office on the death of George I in 1727. Thwarted, the Scriblerians turned to satire to wreak their vengeance. *The Beggar's Opera* began playing to packed audiences at the theatre in Lincoln's Inn Fields on 28 January 1728. Although Gay is supposed to have taken the 'hint' for his 'Newgate pastoral' from Swift, in his calculated comparison of Walpole and the unscrupulous thief-taker, Peachum, he almost seems to have had in mind the passage I have just quoted from from *The Craftsman*. 'A rich Rogue now-a-days is fit Company for any Gentleman', Peachum assures his wife, 'and the World, my Dear, hath not such a Contempt for Roguery as you imagine' (*The Beggar's Opera*, p. 12).

The massive presence of Walpole can be felt lurking behind Gay's burlesque from the moment, right at the beginning of the play, that Peachum reels off a string of nicknames – *Robin* of *Bagshot*, alias *Gorgon*, alias *Bluff Bob*, alias *Carbuncle*, alias *Bob Booty*'. This immediately serves to connect Walpole with the criminal underworld in the mind of the audience, an impression which is reinforced at intervals through repeated innuendoes on the theme of 'great men'. The most notorious moment occurred in the middle of the second act, however, when Peachum and Lockit were discovered, '*with an Account-Book*', discussing the fate of the anti-hero, Macheath:

> *Lock.* In this last Affair, Brother *Peachum*, we are agreed. You have consented to go halves in *Macheath*.
> *Peach.* We shall never fall out about an Execution. – But as to that Article, pray how stands our last Year's account?
> *Lock.* If you will run your Eye over it, you'll find 'tis fair and clearly stated.
> *Peach.* This long Arrear of the Government is very hard upon us! Can it be expected that we should hang our Acquaintants for nothing, when our Betters will hardly save theirs without being paid for it. Unless the People in employment pay better, I promise them for the future, I shall let other Rogues live besides their own.
> *Lock.* Perhaps, Brother, they are afraid these matters may be carried too far. We are treated too by them with Contempt, as if our Profession were not reputable.
> *Peach.* In one respect indeed, our Employment may be reckon'd dishonest, because, like Great Statesmen, we encourage those who betray their Friends.
> *Lock.* Such Language, Brother, any where else, might turn to your prejudice. Learn to be more guarded, I beg you.

> AIR. XII. – How happy are we, *&c.*

> > *When you censure the Age,*
> > *Be cautious and sage,*
> > *Lest the Courtiers offended should be:*
> > *If you mention Vice or Bribe,*
> > *'Tis so pat to all the Tribe;*
> > *Each crys – That was levell'd at me.*

> John Gay, *The Beggar's Opera* (1928), p. 31

'[W]e hear a million of Storys about the opera', Swift wrote to Gay, 'of the ancore [*sic*] at the Song, *That was levelled at me*, when

2 great Ministers were in a Box together, and all the world staring at them' (*Correspondence*, III, 276). For many, Peachum and Lockit discussing their dubious activities resembled nothing so much as Walpole and Townshend, his relative and political henchman, scheming how they could exploit the nation for their own personal gain and, for those among the audience who felt that way, the words of the song clinched it.

According to Gay's Beggar, his opera had a moral:

> *Beg.* Through the whole Piece you may observe such a similitude of Manners in high and low Life, that it is difficult to determine whether (in the fashionable Vices) the fine Gentlemen imitate the Gentlemen of the Road, or the Gentlemen of the Road the fine Gentlemen. – Had the Play remain'd, as I at first intended, it would have carried a most excellent Moral[.] 'Twould have shown that the lower Sort of People have their Vices in a degree as well as the Rich: And that they are punish'd for them.
>
> John Gay, *The Beggar's Opera* (1928), p. 57

In this way the ending to Gay's play was double-edged. Not only did *The Beggar's Opera* implicitly ask its audience to consider who were the bigger rogues, highwaymen or politicians, it heavily dropped the hint that sooner or later corrupt ministers would be brought to account. At the same time it once again drew attention to the failure of those in positions of authority to provide a strong moral lead for the lower orders.

What was insinuated in *The Beggar's Opera* was more or less brought out into the open in *The Dunciad*, however much Pope chose to cloak his work in allegory. Although the world of literature is the ostensible subject-matter of Pope's mock-heroic poem, his representation of the Goddess Dulness who, in the beginning, 'bade *Britannia* sleep, / And pour'd her Spirit o'er the land and deep', is actually making a controversial political point. In asking who is ultimately responsible for legitimising the 'Smithfield Muses', and for bringing them 'to the Ear of Kings', Pope is not simply criticising Walpole and the Hanoverians for failing to patronise writers, or for patronising those who were, in his view, the wrong writers. As it was originally published in

May 1728, *The Dunciad* concluded with a vision of moral bank-
ruptcy which was no less chilling for the mock-heroic diction in
which it was couched:

> Proceed great days! till Learning fly the shore,
> Till Birch shall blush with noble blood no more,
> Till Thames see Eton's sons for ever play,
> Till Westminster's whole year be holiday;
> Till Isis' Elders reel, their Pupils sport;
> And Alma Mater lye dissolv'd in Port!
> Signs following signs lead on the Mighty Year;
> See! the dull stars roll round and re-appear.
> She comes! the Cloud-compelling Pow'r, behold!
> With Night Primæval, and with Chaos old.
> Lo! the great Anarch's ancient reign restor'd,
> Light dies before her uncreating word:
> As one by one, at dread Medæa's strain,
> The sick'ning Stars fade off th' a'thereal plain;
> As Argus' eyes, by Hermes wand opprest,
> Clos'd one by one to everlasting rest;
> Thus at her felt approach, and secret might,
> Art after Art goes out, and all is Night.
> See sculking Truth in her old cavern lye,
> Secur'd by mountains of heap'd casuistry:
> Philosophy, that touch'd the Heavens before,
> Shrinks to her hidden cause, and is no more:
> See Physic beg the Stagyrite's defence!
> See Metaphysic call for aid on Sence!
> See Mystery to Mathematicks fly!
> In vain! they gaze, turn giddy, rave, and die.
> Thy hand great Dulness! lets the curtain fall,
> And universal Darkness covers all.
> Enough! enough! the raptur'd Monarch cries;
> And thro' the Ivory Gate the Vision flies.

Alexander Pope, *The Dunciad Variorum* (1729), pp. 76–9

Although, with Pope going out of his way to settle old scores,
the satire of *The Dunciad* has many targets, it is nonetheless a
perfect illustration of how in the early eighteenth century a
political perspective took in questions of religion and morality.

Pope's vision was one of a society which was progressively losing the ability to distinguish between right and wrong. Rather than a geographical reality, the Empire of Dulness was of course a state of mind, and Pope was targeting its promoters because he believed, or professed to believe, that it was the consequence of a deliberate strategy. Lewis Theobald, the chief dunce of the first version of *The Dunciad*, was not Pope's ultimate target. Nor were the rest of the dunces. In a note to the 1743 edition of his poem Pope revealed who, after all, was the 'true hero' of *The Dunciad*:

> The very *Hero* of the Poem hath been mistaken to this hour; so that we are obliged to open our Notes with a discovery who he really was. We learn from the former Editor, that this Piece was presented by the Hands of Sir Robert Walpole to King George II. Now the author directly tells us, his Hero is the Man
> ———*who brings*
> *The Smithfield Muses to the ear of Kings.*
> And it is notorious who was the person on whom this Prince conferred the honour of the *Laurel* [i.e. Poet Laureate].
>
> It appears as plainly from the *Apostrophe* to the *Great* in the third verse, that Tibbald could not be the person, who was never an Author in fashion, or caressed by the Great; whereas this single characteristic is sufficient to point out the true Hero; who, above all other Poets of his time, was the *Peculiar Delight* and *Chosen Companion* of the Nobility of England; and wrote, as he himself tells us, certain of his Works at the *earnest Desire* of *Persons of Quality.*

Alexander Pope, *The Dunciad, In Four Books* (1743), pp. 40–1

Pope's satirical strategy is to insinuate the existence of a chain of responsibility which can be traced upwards from Colley Cibber to Walpole and finally to George II himself. Cibber was appointed Poet Laureate at Walpole's behest and Pope's syntax contrives to be ambiguous. Who is it who brings the Smithfield Muses to the ear of Kings? Although Cibber is Pope's stalking-horse as 'hero' of *The Dunciad*, it is *Walpole* who actually presents the poem to George II.

Walpole was suspected of nothing less than threatening liberty and property, subverting the social structure and undermining the ancient constitution. Permitting, if not actually promoting, a decline in moral standards was felt to be part of the package. Abuses in religion and learning were perceived as leading to a sort of moral blindness which, in turn, was facilitating the further erosion of the nation's manners. Instead of being governed in the national interest by a natural aristocracy whose wealth and authority were based on land, Britain under the Hanoverians was reckoned to be ruled by upstart, monied men like Walpole who were motivated purely by self-interest.

Walpole was portrayed as a cynical manipulator systematically dismantling or corrupting the old ways. What was alleged to be happening in Parliament was merely the most obvious manifestation of a creeping evil and Walpole was openly accused not only of interfering with the free proceedings of the House of Commons, but with the actual elections themselves. The deleterious constitutional effects of such practices were clearly stated in *The Craftsman*:

> The *Privileges* and *Authority* of that House, (which is no less than the Legislative Power of *all the Commons of England*) is so considerable to every Member of the Community, that the least *Infringement* of them is a common Concern to all.
>
> There have been Times indeed of less Virtue and Integrity than the present, when the *Freedom* or *Independence* of the Members (which is the essential Constitution of that House) has been fatally attempted; but we have this peculiar Happiness, that we can never expect to see it injured or impaired by any Power or Artifice of *evil Ministers*, unless we ourselves should either concur in or connive at them. The *evil Minister* may be the *Tempter*, but the Contagion must become *epidemical*, and the *Corruption universal*, before his Wiles can effectually operate.
>
> There is mention made, by my Lord *Coke*,[7] of a Person, who for 4 *l.* given to the *Mayor*, procured himself to be *returned* a Member of that House, contrary to the *Suffrage of the Burgesses*; but the Patriots of those Times so much resented that dangerous Practice, that the House

thought fit to send the *Mayor* close Prisoner to the *Tower*, and *expelled* the Member with great Indignation; a glorious Example to *future Parliaments*, and which we have seen pursued in so many *modern Instances*, no doubt with the same *Justice*, as well as the same Zeal and Regard for the *Constitution of Parliaments!*

A *County* or *Borough* thus represented, *without their own Consent in a free Election*, cannot be properly said to be *represented at all*, and is thereby excluded its Right in the Legislative OEconomy; so that in respect to *other Parts* of the Nation, it may be said to be in a State of *Slavery*, inasmuch as it has no Share in the *Government*, but is absolutely under the Dominion of *others*; for what is *Slavery* but to be *violently* or *fraudulently* divested of that Share of Power to which a Man is legally entitled; or, which is the same thing, to be *subject to the absolute Power of another?*

Could we suppose, that, at the time mentioned by my Lord *Coke*, there had been a *Majority of such Persons* return'd to Parliament, by the general Corruption of the *Returning Officers*, there can be no doubt that whoever had apply'd for Redress to it would have met with the greatest Discouragement, and *such Members*, by countenancing one another, would have established their Seats there; and then, where would have been the *Commons of England?* – it is plain they could not have been presumed to be duly represented by such an *usurped Authority*.

A *Corruption*, of this Nature, would not have ended there; I mean in merely establishing themselves; for if they had any *Views* of their own to carry on, they would have had it likewise in their Power (being now, by their *Majority*, become sole Judges *of Elections*) to remove any *Person*, who They might imagine would oppose their *destructive Scheme* and introduce *others*, who they knew would co-operate with them. Indeed many wholesome Laws have been since made to support the *Freedom of Elections*, and a constant Adherence to them gives us no Prospect of such a Violation of our Constitution.

And yet such a *general Corruption*, as I have above supposed, is not merely so fantastical as one would at first imagine, by looking into the present Frame and Composition of that House, and observing the universal Abhorrence of any *indirect Means* to obtain a Seat there, as well as the inevitable Expulsion of those, who make such an Attempt; for you was pleased, in one of your Papers, to mention a *great Man* in that House, who formerly boasted, that he was just come from voting *the minor Number to be the Majority*; than which one would imagine there could not be a greater Instance of *Corruption*, as it tends to efface the first Rudiments of common Honesty and common Sense. Such an Abuse to the Understanding of Mankind could not easily be believed, did not History too well attest the Possibility; and indeed, what else can be expected from such a *venal, sordid Majority*; for such they must be who willingly are led blindfold, to pursue the irregular Temper and Passions of *some great Minister?* but our own happy Times are not only free from such Abuses, but they have been discountenanced and exploded in so vigorous a Manner, that we hope they will never revive.

The Craftsman No. 111: 17 August 1728

Like the 'moral' of *The Beggar's Opera*, this was a warning shot across Walpole's bows. Under the first two Georges the ministry did indeed control the Committee of Privileges and Elections, using it as a means to increase the number of its supporters in the Commons by displacing its opponents and replacing them with those likely to vote for the government. Significantly, the first real sign that Walpole's days were numbered was when in December 1741 the opposition managed for the only time hitherto in the eighteenth century to place its candidate in the chair of the Committee of Privileges and Elections in the teeth of the government.

The essay I have just quoted illustrates characteristic opposition ploys. It became *The Craftsman*'s habitual practice, for instance, to compare the conduct of unscrupulous characters from the annals of history with their alleged modern counterparts. Thus, in accordance with the editor's 'ancient Method of defaming by *Parallel History*', Walpole was likened to a series of traitors and malefactors while the characters of the latter were 'rack'd and tortur'd, to make them agree' with the 'political Standard' of the opposition (*Free Briton* No. 124: 13 April 1732).

Another common tactic was the ironic insistence that, although there had indeed been times 'of less Virtue and Integrity than the present', liberty and property were bound to be safe in the hands of those currently holding positions of power and responsibility. Sometimes, however, it was effective to do away with the irony altogether and offer an ostensibly straightforward comparison of degenerate modern times with those bygone days when virtue and integrity still persisted in England. Swift employs both techniques when he arranges for Gulliver, in Glubbdubdrib, to summon the spirits of the dead. Not surprisingly, Gulliver's requests have a political point to make:

> I had the Curiosity to enquire in a particular manner, by what Method great Numbers had procured to themselves high Titles of Honour, and prodigious Estates; and I confined my Enquiry to a very modern Period: however without grating upon present Times, because I would be sure to give no Offence even to Foreigners, (for I hope the Reader need not be told that I do not in the least intend my own Country in what I say upon this Occasion) a great number of Persons concerned were called up, and upon a very slight Examination, discovered such a Scene of Infamy, that I cannot reflect upon it without some Seriousness [. . .] As every Person called up made exactly the same appearance he had done in the World, it gave me melancholy Reflections to observe how much the Race of human kind was degenerate among us, within these hundred Years past. How the Pox under all its Consequences and Denominations had altered every Lineament of an *English* Countenance, shortned the size of Bodies, unbraced the Nerves, relaxed the Sinews and Muscles, introduced a sallow Complexion, and rendered the Flesh loose and *Rancid.*
>
> I descended so low as to desire that some *English* Yeoman of the old stamp, might be summoned to appear, once so famous for the Simplicity of their Manners, Dyet and Dress, for Justice in their Dealings, for their true Spirit of Liberty, for their Valour and Love

of their Country. Neither could I be wholly unmov'd after comparing the Living with the Dead, when I considered how all these pure native Virtues were prostituted for a piece of Money by their Grand-children, who in selling their Votes, and managing at Elections have acquired every Vice and Corruption that can possibly be learned in a Court.

Jonathan Swift, *Gulliver's Travels*, Part III, pp. 112–17

The opposition's vision of an upright, paternalistic ruling class was of course a myth; the propertied wished to protect their privileged position and the best way to defend it from threats from below was to hedge it around with religious and ideological safeguards. Myths are powerful nevertheless, and the satirists, especially Pope, were careful to temper their attacks on the system of Walpole with the positive enunciation of their own ideal. What they needed to explain, above all, was why so much power and wealth was concentrated in the hands of so few. This was of course one of the major themes of Pope's *Essay on Man*, that vast ideological symphony of complacency leading to the thunderous climax, ' "Whatever IS, is RIGHT" ':

> ORDER is Heav'n's first law; and this confest,
> Some are, and must be, greater than the rest,
> More rich, more wise; but who infers from hence
> That such are happier, shocks all common sense.
> Heav'n to Mankind impartial we confess,
> If all are equal in their Happiness:
> But mutual wants this Happiness increase,
> All Nature's diff'rence keeps all Nature's peace.
> Condition, circumstance is not the thing;
> Bliss is the same in subject or in king,
> In who obtain defence, or who defend,
> In him who is, or him who finds a friend:
> Heav'n breathes thro' ev'ry member of the whole
> One common blessing, as one common soul.
> But Fortune's gifts if each alike possest,
> And each were equal, must not all contest?
> If then to all Men Happiness was meant,
> God in Externals could not place Content.

Fortune her gifts may variously dispose,
And these be happy call'd, unhappy those;
But Heav'n's just balance equal will appear,
While those are plac'd in Hope, and these in Fear:
Not present good or ill, the joy or curse,
But future views of better, or of worse.
    Oh sons of earth! attempt ye still to rise,
By mountains pil'd on mountains, to the skies?
Heav'n still with laughter the vain toil surveys,
And buries madmen in the heaps they raise.

Alexander Pope, *An Essay on Man* (1743), pp. 85–7

After completing the first version of *The Dunciad* Pope had turned to writing 'Horatian' epistles addressed to exemplary contemporaries. In the *Epistle to Burlington* we are not only offered an extended caricature of the type of self-interested, unworthy landlord who was alleged to flourish in the age of Walpole, but Pope rounds off his poem with a fine section in which he manages to include a critique of Timon the misanthrope, an affirmation of the beneficent workings of Providence, a sketch of the truly virtuous landlord, an apostrophe to the model architect, Richard Boyle, Earl of Burlington, and an appeal to George II to exert himself to put things right.

The poet spends a day at Timon's villa, and witnesses the huge sums which are vainly spent by Timon on luxury and pleasure instead of virtue and benevolence. On the surface, Timon's conduct seems a mockery of a social system founded on deference and dependence – until Pope employs paradox to striking effect. Timon may be a wastrel without taste; he may, indeed, care little for those subordinates whom he is supposed to protect:

Yet hence the Poor are cloath'd, the Hungry fed;
Health to himself, and to his Infants bread
The Lab'rer bears: What his hard Heart denies,
His charitable Vanity supplies.
    Another age shall see the golden Ear
Imbrown the Slope, and nod on the Parterre,
Deep Harvests bury all his pride has plann'd,
And laughing Ceres re-assume the land.

Who then shall grace, or who improve the Soil?
Who plants like BATHURST,[8] or who builds like BOYLE.
'Tis Use alone that sanctifies Expence,
And Splendor borrows all her rays from Sense.

His Father's Acres who enjoys in peace,
Or makes his Neighbours glad, if he encrease;
Whose chearful Tenants bless their yearly toil,
Yet to their Lord owe more than to the soil;
Whose ample Lawns are not asham'd to feed
The milky heifer and deserving steed;
Whose rising Forests, not for pride or show,
But future Buildings, future Navies grow;
Let his plantations stretch from down to down,
First shade a Country, and then raise a Town.

You too proceed! make falling Arts your care,
Erect new wonders, and the old repair,
Jones and Palladio to themselves restore,
And be whate'er Vitruvius was before:
Till Kings call forth th'Idea's of your mind,
Proud to accomplish what such hands design'd,
Bid Harbors open, public Ways extend,
Bid Temples, worthier of the God, ascend;
Bid the broad Arch the dang'rous Flood contain,
The Mole projected break the roaring Main;
Back to his bounds their subject Sea command,
And roll obedient Rivers thro' the Land;
These Honours, Peace to happy Britain brings,
These are Imperial Works, and worthy Kings.

Alexander Pope, *Epistles to Several Persons* (1743), pp. 92–3

Many things might be said about this splendid passage, which concludes with a reformulation of the idea of the Great Chain of Being in which even rivers 'roll obedient [. . .] thro' the Land', a concept which Pope also exploits in the *Essay on Man*:

God, in the nature of each being, founds
Its proper bliss, and sets its proper bounds:
But as he fram'd a Whole, the Whole to bless,
On mutual Wants built mutual Happiness:
So from the first eternal ORDER ran,

And creature link'd to creature, man to man.
Whate'er of life all-quick'ning æther keeps,
Or breathes thro' air, or shoots beneath the deeps,
Or pours profuse on earth; one nature feeds
The vital flame, and swells the genial seeds.

Alexander Pope, *An Essay on Man* (1743), pp. 60–1

Above all, however, the *Epistle to Burlington* once again draws attention to the contemporary connection between manners and morals. In the hands of men like Timon a dangerous disjunction can be seen taking place, the social consequences of which could not be assessed. The poem recalls the political vision of *Windsor-Forest* and might be seen as a last, desperate plea for the founding of a new Golden Age where actions and ideals would somehow coincide.

But George II did not call on Burlington or his ideas. By 1737 Pope had given up and was publishing the vitriolic *Epistle to Augustus*:

WHile You, great Patron of Mankind, sustain
The balanc'd World, and open all the Main;
Your Country, chief, in Arms abroad defend,
At home, with Morals, Arts, and Laws amend;
How shall the Muse, from such a Monarch, steal
An hour, and not defraud the Publick Weal?

Dripping with sustained irony, Pope's poem uses Dryden's tactic of blame by praise, for the *Epistle to Augustus* is ostensibly an encomium of George Augustus:

To Thee, the World its present homage pays,
The Harvest early, but mature the Praise:
Great Friend of LIBERTY! in *Kings* a Name
Above all Greek, above all Roman Fame:
Whose Word is Truth, as sacred and rever'd,
As Heav'n's own Oracles from Altars heard.
Wonder of Kings! like whom, to mortal eyes
None e'er has risen, and none e'er shall rise.

Alexander Pope, *Poems, and Imitations of Horace*
(1738), pp. 5, 7–9

Other writers had already turned to strident criticism of the Hanoverian Court. In *On Poetry: A Rapsody*, a poem which in many ways is Swift's *Dunciad*, the oblique mode of attack of the *Epistle to Augustus* had been anticipated by the writer who claimed, in mock seriousness, to have been 'born to introduce' irony:

> Fair *Britain* in thy Monarch blest,
> Whose Virtues bear the strictest Test;
> Whom never *Faction* cou'd bespatter,
> Nor *Minister*, nor *Poet* flatter.
> What Justice in rewarding Merit?
> What Magnanimity of Spirit?
> What Lineaments divine we trace
> Thro' all the Features of his Face;
> Tho' Peace with Olive bind his Hands,
> Confest the conqu'ring Hero stands.
> *Hydaspes, Indus*, and the *Ganges*,
> Dread from his Hand impending Changes.
> From him the *Tartar*, and *Chinese*,
> Short by the Knees intreat for Peace.
> The *Consort* of his Throne and Bed,
> A perfect Goddess born and bred.
> Appointed sov'reign Judge to sit
> On Learning, Eloquence and Wit.
> Our eldest Hope, divine *Iülus*,
> (Late, very late, O, may he rule us.)
> What early Manhood has he shown,
> Before his downy Beard was grown!
> Then think, what Wonders will be done
> By going on as he begun;
> An Heir for *Britain* to secure
> As long as Sun and Moon endure.

Jonathan Swift, *On Poetry: A Rapsody* (1733), pp. 24–5

In Swift's swingeing satire on the entire royal family – George II, Queen Caroline, and their offspring, especially Frederick Louis, Prince of Wales – not even the Great Man himself was spared:

Now sing the *Minister* of *State*,
Who shines alone, without a Mate.
Observe with what majestick Port
This *Atlas* stands to prop the Court:
Intent the Publick Debts to pay,
Like prudent *Fabius* by *Delay*.
Thou great Viceregent of the King,
Thy Praises ev'ry Muse shall sing.
In all Affairs thou sole Director,
Of Wit and Learning chief Protector;
Tho' small the Time thou hast to spare,
The Church is thy peculiar Care.
Of pious Prelates what a Stock
You chuse to rule the Sable-flock.
You raise the Honour of the Peerage,
Proud to attend you at the Steerage.
You dignify the noble Race,
Content yourself with humbler Place.

Jonathan Swift, *On Poetry: A Rapsody* (1733), pp. 25–6

In his earlier 'Directions for a Birth-day Song', Swift had explained how to write the sort of panegyric which was regularly being turned out by Court sycophants. The knack was to praise members of the royal family and the administration for characteristics which they conspicuously lacked. *On Poetry: A Rapsody* was a brilliant ironic demonstration of how this should be done:

Say, Poet, in what other Nation,
Shone ever such a Constellation.
Attend ye *Popes*, and *Youngs*, and *Gays*,
And tune your Harps, and strow your Bays.
Your Panegyricks here provide,
You cannot err on Flatt'ry's Side.
Above the Stars exalt your Stile,
You still are low ten thousand Mile.

Jonathan Swift, *On Poetry: A Rapsody* (1733), pp. 26–7

Swift, as ever, had chosen to employ a dangerous tactic. His remarks, although couched in irony, were much too strong to pass unnoticed. A number of those involved in the publication of the poem were arrested, including Swift's friend, Mrs Barber, who had carried the manuscript to London. For whatever reason none was actually prosecuted. Perhaps the government thought it was too delicate a matter to pursue; perhaps it was believed that a warning would be enough. If the latter, then it was no more than a pious hope. The flow of pointed commentaries on the state of the nation under George II and his prime minister, Walpole, continued unabated.

By no means all of them were done in the ironic manner of the Scriblerians. James Thomson employed a high poetic style rather than humour. He first drew attention to the contemporary threat to liberty in *Britannia* (1729), published in the same year as *The Dunciad Variorum*, which anticipated the implied connection between the moral and spiritual well-being of the nation and the lead offered by the Crown which Pope was to make in the *Epistle to Burlington*:

> OH let not then waste *Luxury* impair
> That manly Soul of Toil, which strongs your Nerves,
> And your own proper Happiness creates!
> Oh let not the soft, penetrating Plague
> Creep on the free-born Mind! And working there,
> With the sharp Tooth of many a new-form'd Want,
> Endless, and idle all, eat out the Heart
> Of LIBERTY; the high Conception blast;
> The noble Sentiment, th' impatient Scorn
> Of base Subjection, and the swelling Wish
> For general Good, erazing from the Mind:
> While nought save narrow *Selfishness* succeeds,
> And low Design, the gloomy Passions all
> Let loose, and reigning in the rankled Breast.
> Induc'd at last, by scarce-perceiv'd Degrees,
> Sapping the very Frame of Government,
> And Life, total *Dissolution* comes:
> Sloth, Ignorance, Dejection, Flattery, Fear,
> Oppression raging o'er the Waste He makes;
> The human Being almost quite extinct;
> And the whole State in broad *Corruption* sinks.
> Oh shun that Gulph! That gaping Ruin shun!
> And countless Ages roll it far away

From you, ye Heaven-belov'd! may LIBERTY,
The Light of Life! the Sun of human kind!
Whence *Heroes, Bards,* and *Patriots* borrow Flame,
Even where the keen depressive *North* descends,
Still spread, exalt, and actuate your Powers!
While slavish *Southern* Climates beam in vain.
And may a *publick* Spirit from the THRONE,
Where every *Virtue* sits, go copious forth
Wide o'er the Land! the *finer Arts* inspire;
Make thoughtful *Science* raise his pensive Head,
Blow the fresh *Bay,* bid *Industry* rejoice,
And the rough *Sons* of lowest *Labour* smile.

James Thomson, *Britannia* (1729), pp. 14–15

A year later in the first complete edition of *The Seasons* Thomson
added a section to *Summer* which extolled the virtues of a list of
British patriots. Conspicuous among these was 'the British
Cassius', Algernon Sidney. Having nailed his colours firmly to
the opposition mast, Thomson set to work on a five-part poem
actually called *Liberty,* which made its appearance the same year
as Pope's *Epistle to Augustus.*

On VIRTUE *can alone* MY KINGDOM *stand,*
On PUBLICK VIRTUE, EVERY VIRTUE JOIN'D.
For, lost this social Cement of Mankind,
The greatest Empires, by scarce-felt Degrees,
Will moulder soft away; 'till, tottering loose,
They prone at last to total Ruin rush.
Unblest by VIRTUE, *Government* a *League*
Becomes, a *circling Junto of the Great,*
To rob by Law; *Religion* mild a *Yoke*
To tame the stooping Soul, a *Trick of State*
To mask their Rapine, and to share the Prey.
What are without IT *Senates,* save a Face
Of Consultation deep and Reason free,
While the determin'd Voice and Heart are sold?
What boasted *Freedom,* save a sounding Name?
And what *Election,* but a Market vile
Of Slaves self-barter'd? VIRTUE! without THEE,
There is no ruling Eye, no Nerve, in States;

War has no Vigour, and no Safety Peace:
Even Justice warps to Party, Laws oppress,
Wide thro' the Land their weak Protection fails,
First broke the Ballance, and then scorn'd the Sword.
Thus Nations sink, Society dissolves;
Rapine and Guile and Violence break loose,
Everting Life, and turning Love to Gall;
Man hates the Face of Man, and *Indian* Woods
And *Lybia*'s hissing Sands to him are tame.
    By those THREE VIRTUES be the Frame sustain'd,
Of BRITISH FREEDOM: INDEPENDENT LIFE;
INTEGRITY IN OFFICE: and, o'er all
Supreme, A PASSION FOR THE COMMON-WEAL.

James Thomson, *The Prospect: Being the Fifth Part of Liberty*
(1736), pp. 9–11

What is striking about Thomson's impassioned paean to liberty is the way in which it contrives to encompass the ideological debates of the previous sixty years or more in its insinuation that, without virtue, religion will be regarded as simply 'a *Trick of State*', society will degenerate into anarchy, and man will shun the company of man. We are back to Rochester and Hobbes.

Walpole and the Hanoverian Court were being attacked in prose and in verse, in avowed works of fiction and in newspapers and periodicals. Perhaps the climax of this sustained assault came in 1737, not with Pope's *Epistle to Augustus*, but with two notorious issues of a new periodical called *Common Sense: Or, The Englishman's Journal* that used the (by now) hackneyed vehicle of dream allegory to attack George II as the 'Golden Rump'. The narrator of the dream vision visits 'the annual Festival of the GOLDEN RUMP', where he encounters an idol resembling a pagod (the homophone – 'pay-god' – is, I suspect, far from accidental):

This IDOL was an human Figure, excepting only that he had Goats Legs and Feet, like those which are given by Poets and Statuaries to the old *Satyrs*. His Head was made of Wood, his Body down to the Waist of Silver; and his Posteriors, which were large and prominent, and from whence he derived his Title, were of solid Gold. By this Description the Reader may easily conceive that the Back of the IDOL was turned to the Congregation; an Attitude which I do not remember to have observed among the *Chinese* and *Indian Pagods*. But my friendly Conductor informed me, that he had placed himself in this Posture upon his first Entrance into the Temple, as well as to shew his Politeness, as to testify his Respect and Gratitude to a Nation which had elected him into the Number of the *Diu majories*, or *greater Gods*. Here I could not help smiling, to think how widely the Custom of this Country differed from mine, where the same Thing, which passed here for Civility and good Manners, would be reckoned a Mark of Insolence and Brutality.

But to proceed in my Vision – On the Right-Hand of the PAGOD stood the TAPANTA (for so the HIGH-PRIESTESS was styled) dress'd in the Habit of a *Roman* Matron [Queen Caroline]. Her *Stola*, or upper Garment, was of Gold Brocade, adorned with Diamonds and other Jewels. She had a Silver Bell in one Hand, and a small Golden Pipe or Tube in the other, with a large Bag or Bladder at the end of it. It exactly resembled a common Clyster-pipe, and was used, as my Friend explained it to me, in the same manner. For the Bladder was full of *Aurum potabile* [liquid gold], compounded with Pearl Powders, and other choice Ingredients. This Medicine, at proper Seasons, was injected by the TAPANTA into the F[un]d[amen]t of the PAGOD, to comfort his Bowels, and preserve his Complexion. It was likewise applied, upon extraordinary Occasions, to appease the IDOL, when he lifted up his cloven Foot to correct his Domesticks who officiated at the Altar. However, as he was naturally very cholerick, so his Fury was sometimes so very sudden and unexpected, that he imprinted visible Marks of it on all who stood near him, ere the HIGH-PRIESTESS had time to apply the golden Clyster. And sometimes the Storm was so loud and violent, and the PRIESTESS met with such Opposition in those Parts to which she directed her Tube [. . .] that she was unable to apply it at all, at least with any Success. But these unnatural Sallies or Hurricanes had not happened, as my Conductor assured me, above two or three times since the Deification of the PAGOD; and only then, when his Godship was deeply smitten with the Charms of a mortal Dame.

Common Sense (1738), I, 49–50

Once again the legacy of *Gulliver's Travels* is readily apparent, as a contrast between English manners and those of another fictitious society is made for satirical effect. The 'Golden Rump' papers also imitate Swift's scatological approach. While the allegory could hardly be accused of subtlety, it was certainly apposite. Crudely, the suggestion was that the Hanoverians, with Walpole's connivance, were shitting on the nation. Walpole was portrayed as 'the CHIEF MAGICIAN', 'called GASTER ARGOS, being thus denominated from his Belly, which was as large and prominent as the PAGOD's rump'. Like Swift's Sid Hamet, this magician also possessed a rod of 'marvellous Virtue', the Lord Treasurer's staff of office, and there was 'an ancient Prophecy or Tradition which prevailed throughout the Land, that the GOLDEN RUMP should continue in the Fulness of his Glory, and the HIGH-PRIESTESS and GASTER maintain their Authority, as long as the latter possessed that Rod; which could never be destroyed or eaten up, but by the Rod of *Aaron*' (*Common Sense*, I, 51).

Rumours abounded in 1737 that the 'Golden Rump' papers were about to be translated on to the stage. The threat was headed off in the same year by the theatrical Licensing Act, which required material to be submitted for official approval before it could be staged. Perhaps, as far as Walpole was concerned, the thought of being portrayed on stage as the Gaster Argos was the final straw. He had already, after all, 'suffer[ed] himself to be produced for thirty nights together upon the stage in the person of a highwayman' during *The Beggar's Opera*'s record-breaking run (Hervey, *Memoirs of the Reign of George II*, I, 98).

From the 1720s onwards, then, the royal family and the Great Man had been subjected to a variety of methods of ridicule and abuse on stage. Prominent among their detractors was Henry Fielding, who was reputed to have been involved in the dramatic adaptation of the 'Golden Rump' papers. In *The Historical Register for the Year 1736*, however, Fielding exploited the 'rehearsal' formula to satirise both Walpole *and* the opposition 'patriots'. Although the play ostensibly being rehearsed is about the state of Corsica, it scarcely needs to be said that it is actually about the state of the nation under Walpole who, under an alias, is standing behind the scenes watching the antics of the so-called patriots who oppose him:

> *Sour.* Why do you suffer that Actor to stand laughing behind the Scenes, and interrupt your Rehearsal?
> *Med.* O, Sir, he ought to be there; he's a-laughing in his Sleeve at the Patriots; he's a very considerable Character – and has much to do by-and-by.
> *Sour.* Methinks the Audience should know that, or perhaps they may mistake him as I did, and hiss him.
> *Med.* If they shou'd, he's a pure impudent Fellow, and can stand the Hisses of them all; I chose him particularly for the Part – Go on, Patriots.
> 1 *Patr.* Gentlemen, I think this our Island of *Corsica* is a[n] ill State; I do not say we are actually in War, for that we are not; but, however, we are threaten'd with it daily, and why may not the Apprehension of a War, like other Evils, be worse than the Evil itself? For my Part, this I will say, this I will venture to say, That let what will happen, I will drink a Health to Peace.
> *Med.* This Gentleman is the Noisy Patriot, who drinks and roars for his Country, and never does either Good or Harm in it – The next is the Cautious Patriot.
> 2 *Patr.* Sir, give me your Hand; there's Truth in what you say, and I will pledge you with all my Soul, but remember it is all under the Rose.
> 3 *Patr.* Look'ee, Gentlemen, my Shop is my Country; I always measure the Prosperity of the latter by that of the former. My Country is either richer or poorer, in my Opinion, as my Trade rises or falls; therefore, Sir, I cannot agree with you that a War wou'd be disserviceable: On the contrary, I think it the only Way to make my Country flourish; for as I am a Sword-Cutler, it would make my Shop flourish, so here's to War.
> *Med.* This is the Self-interested Patriot, and now you shall hear the fourth and last Kind, which is the Indolent

Patriot, one who acts as I have seen a prudent Man in company, fall asleep at the Beginning of a Fray, and never wake till the End on't.

4 *Patr.* Here's to Peace or War, I do not care which.

Sour. So this Gentleman being neutral, Peace has it two to one.

Med. Perhaps neither shall have it; perhaps I have found a Way to reconcile both Parties: But go on.

1 *Patr.* Can any one, who is a Friend to *Corsica*, wish for War, in our present Circumstances? – I desire to ask you all one Question, Are we not a Set of miserable poor Dogs?

Omnes. Ay, ay.

3 *Patr.* That we are, sure enough; that no body will deny.

Enter Quidam.

Quid. Yes, Sir, I deny it. [*All start*] Nay, Gentlemen, let me not disturb you, I beg you will all sit down. I am come to drink a Glass with you – Can *Corsica* be poor while there is this in it? [*Lays a Purse on the Table*] Nay, be not afraid of it, Gentlemen, it is honest gold, I assure you; you are a Set of poor Dogs, you agree, I say you are not, for this is all yours, there, [*Pours it on the Table*] take it among you.

1 *Patr.* And what are we to do for it?

Quid. Only say you are rich, that's all.

Omnes. Oh, if that be all! [*They snatch up the Money.*

Quid. Well, Sir, what is your Opinion now? Tell me freely.

1 *Patr.* I will. A Man may be in the Wrong through Ignorance, but he's a Rascal, who speaks with open Eyes against his Conscience – I own I thought we were poor, but, Sir, you have convinced me that we are rich.

Omnes. We are all convinc'd.

Quid. Then you are all honest Fellows, and here is to your Healths, and since the Bottle is out, hang Sorrow, cast away Care, e'en take a Dance, and I will play you a Tune on the Fiddle.

Omnes. Agreed.

1 *Patr.* Strike up when you will, we are ready to attend your Motions.
[*Dance here*; Quidam *dances out, and they all dance after him.*]

Henry Fielding, *The Historical Register for the Year 1736* (1737),
pp. 25–7

Thus the so-called patriots are led a merry dance by Walpole, *alias* Quidam, who, through the timely application of specie, ensures that the opposition, for all its bluster, will vote in the Commons for those motions moved by the government.

Fielding was fond of using the inversion of normal values to make a satirical point in his prose fiction, too. In the same way that Walpole was habitually yet ironically called 'the Great Man' by opposition writers, so Fielding in *The Life of Mr. Jonathan Wild the Great* questions contemporary usage of terms like '*great*' and '*honest*' in the light of the Prime Minister's dubious political activities, as he explained at length in the Preface to his *Miscellanies*:

> I think we may be excused for suspecting, that the splendid Palaces of the Great are often no other than *Newgate* with the Mask on. Nor do I know any thing which can raise an honest Man's Indignation higher than that the same Morals should be in one Place attended with all imaginable Misery and Infamy, and in the other, with the highest Luxury and Honour. Let any impartial Man in his Senses be asked, for which of these two Places a Composition of Cruelty, Lust, Avarice, Rapine, Insolence, Hypocrisy, Fraud and Treachery, was best fitted, surely his Answer must be certain and immediate; and yet I am afraid all these Ingredients glossed over with Wealth and a Title, have been treated with the highest Respect and Veneration in the one, while one or two of them have been condemned to the Gallows in the other.
>
> If there are any Men of such Morals who dare to call themselves Great, and are so reputed, or called at least, by the deceived Multitude, surely a little private Censure by the few is a very moderate Tax for them to pay, provided

no more was to be demanded: But I fear this is not the Case [. . . .]

Nothing seems to me more preposterous than that, while the Way to true Honour lies so open and plain, Men should seek false by such perverse and rugged Paths: that while it is so easy and safe, and truly honourable, to be good, Men should wade through Difficulty and Danger, and real Infamy, to be *Great*, or, to use a synonimous Word, *Villains.*

Nor hath Goodness less Advantage in the Article of Pleasure, than of Honour over this kind of Greatness [. . . .]

But perhaps some Apology may be required of me, for having used the Word *Greatness*, to which the World have affixed such honourable Ideas, in so disgraceful and contemptuous a Light. Now if the Fact be, that the Greatness which is commonly worshipped is really of the Kind which I have here represented, the Fault seems rather to lie in those who have ascribed it to those Honours, to which it hath not in Reality the least Claim.

The Truth, I apprehend is, we often confound the Ideas of Goodness and Greatness together, or rather include the former in our Idea of the latter. If this be so, it is surely a great Error, and no less than a Mistake of the Capacity for the Will. In Reality, no Qualities can be more distinct: for as it cannot be doubted but that Benevolence, Honour, Honesty, and Charity, make a good Man; and that Parts, Courage, are the efficient Qualities of a Great Man, so must it be confess'd, that the Ingredients which compose the former of these Characters, bear no Analogy to, nor Dependence on those which constitute the latter. A Man may therefore be Great without being Good, or Good without being Great.

Henry Fielding, *Miscellanies* (1743), I, xx–xxvi

Like Gay in *The Beggar's Opera*, Fielding was drawing parallels more or less openly between the way in which Walpole was running the country, and the way in which the real-life thief-taker and racketeer, Jonathan Wild, had operated his system of organised crime. Fielding insisted, quite rightly, that his *Life* was 'not a very faithful Portrait of *Jonathan Wild* himself'. Less convincing was his insistence that it was not 'intended to represent the Features of any other Person' either. 'Roguery, and not a Rogue, is my Subject', he maintained somewhat disingenuously, the comparison with Walpole being obvious.

Although evidence of the nation's moral degeneracy during Walpole's long tenure of office does not appear overwhelming, contemporaries were certain that a decline in standards was taking place. Johnson compared the situation under Walpole with the alleged situation under King Alfred:

> Scarce can our Fields, such Crowds at *Tyburn* die,
> With Hemp the Gallows and the Fleet supply.
> Propose your Schemes, ye Senatorian Band.
> Whose Ways and Means support the sinking Land;
> Lest Ropes be wanting in the tempting Spring,
> To rig another Convoy for the K[in]g.
> A single Jail, in ALFRED's golden Reign,
> Could half the Nation's Criminals contain;
> Fair Justice then, without Constraint ador'd,
> Sustain'd the Ballance, but resign'd the Sword;
> No Spies were paid, no *Special Juries* known,
> Blest Age! But ah! how diff'rent from our own!

> Samuel Johnson, *London* (1738), p. 18

Yet despite all the dissatisfaction constantly being expressed in print, Walpole continued to cling on to office – despite the death of George I in 1727, despite being forced to back down in the teeth of a concerted opposition campaign against his excise scheme in 1733, despite Frederick, the Prince of Wales, going into opposition in 1737 after quarrelling with his father, George II, and therefore providing a focal point around which those disaffected with the ministry might gather.

Walpole spent over £50,000 funding an expensive counter-propaganda campaign in the last ten years of his ministry, yet, as *Common Sense* was at pains to point out, all the good writers were on the opposition side:

> This certainly never happen'd in any Reign, or under any

Administration before; for, excepting a late Imitation of *Horace* [the *Epistle to Augustus*], by Mr. *Pope*, who but seldom meddles with publick Matters, I challenge the Ministerial Advocates to produce one Line of *Sense*, or *English*, written on their side of the Question for these last Seven Years. – Has any one Person of distinguish'd eminency, in any one Art or Science, shown the least Tendency to support or defend 'em? – Has there been an Essay, in Verse or Prose, has there been even a Distich, or an Advertisement, fit to be read, on the Side of the Administration? – But on the other side, what Numbers of Dissertations, Essays, Treatises, Compositions of all Kinds, in Verse and Prose, have been written, with all that Strength of Reasoning, Quickness of Wit, and Elegancy of Expression, which no former Period of Time can equal? – Has not every body got by heart, Satires, Lampoons, Ballads, and Sarcasms against the Administration? And can any body recollect, or repeat one Line for it? What can be the Cause of this? It cannot be, that those who are able to serve the honourable Person, despair of being rewarded by him, since the known Instances of his Liberality, to the worst Writers, are sure Pledges of his Profusion to the best. – Is it then the rigid Virtue, the inflexible Honour of the brightest Genius's of this Age, that hinders 'em from ingaging in that Cause, for which they would be so amply recompens'd? If so, I congratulate the present Times, for that was not usually the Characteristick of Wit; and they were formerly accus'd of Flattery, at least, if not of Prostitution, to ministerial Favour and Rewards.

In all the former Reigns, the Wits were of the Side of the Ministers [. . . .]

Common Sense (1738), pp. 247–8

On their own, however, the wits were unable to topple the Great Man, for the reasons given by the opposition journal, *The Champion*: 'WRITINGS, Gentlemen, may serve to discover Leaks in the Common-wealth, but want Power to stop them' (*The Champion* (1741), Preface).

What was required was effective political pressure, and this the

opposition seemed singularly unable to supply. Fielding had
already ridiculed the motives of the 'patriots' in *The Historical
Register*, as we have seen; by the parliamentary session of 1741–42
he was prepared to question the very basis of the opposition case
against Walpole:

> Methought I was walking in the High-way, not far from
> *London*, where *I met the* OPPOSITION, a Phrase which may
> at first puzzle the Reader [. . .] It was a Waggon extremely
> heavy laden, and (which surprized me greatly) was drawn
> by *Asses* instead of Horses; the Asses were of different
> Colours and Sizes, and so extremely ill matched, that the
> whole made the most ridiculous Appearance imaginable
> [. . .] An immense Number of Persons on Foot, who all
> seemed of the *Mobile* Order [i.e. the lower orders],
> attended it with frequent Huzzas. I suddenly stopt at this
> strange Sight, expecting it to approach me; but finding,
> at last, that, instead of moving forwards, it *stood quite still*,
> I walked up to the Asses, when one of the Drivers (for
> there were several) asked Me, *which was his Way?* Whither,
> Sir, cry'd I? to which he returned no Answer: But a
> Passenger from the Waggon, seeing me look surprized,
> told me plainly, he believed the Driver *scarce knew himself
> whither he was going*. For his Part, he honestly confest he
> did not; he added, the Waggon had stood still so long
> that he was extremely *cold*, and began to despair of ever
> seeing it *move again*. I now surveyed this strange Vehicle
> all round; it's Lading seemed to be chiefly a vast Trunk,
> on which was inscribed the Word GRIEVANCES, and a
> huge BOX with PUBLIC SPIRIT written in large golden
> Characters on it's *Outside*; these were so placed, that they
> seemed contrived to catch the Eye of every Beholder;
> there was another large Trunk tied behind, which had
> nothing written on it, but contained, as I was whispered
> *Motions for the Year* 1741–2, on which rode an ill-look'd
> Fellow, carrying a large Flag; the Waggon was, besides,
> full of a great Number of passengers, who sat *Back to
> Back*, and (which was very remarkable) *scarce two of them
> looked the same Way*. I observed moreover, many of them
> distinguished by *white Roses* in their Hats, others by
> *red*, and no small Number of a sour Complection, with-

out *any Rose at all.* Whilst I was thus entertained, several from behind called aloud to the Head-Carter to *go on*, and others in the fore part of the Waggon gave, at the same Time, different Directions, some bidding him drive *to the Right*, some to the *Left*, and some calling to him to *move directly* forwards, without regarding *the Dirtiness of the Way*. He answered, he only waited for *a fresh Supply of Asses*, and then intended to drive *through thick and thin*; for he was obliged to pass such abominable bad Ways, that it would required immense Strength to drag them through.

Henry Fielding, *The Opposition. A Vision* (1742), pp. 4–7

When examined, the 'vast Trunk' containing the opposition's grievances turned out to be virtually empty:

> to my great Surprize, [it] contained little more than a few News-papers, on one of which I read the Word *Champion*, and on another was the Word *onsense*, the Letter *N* being, I suppose, folded down; there were indeed one or two little Parcels at the *Bottom*, which seemed to have something in them; they appeared however *fastened* to the Trunk, and my Friend told me, were not intended to be removed by any there, when they came to their Journey's End. I observed they were directed to the same Person, at his House in *Downing-Street*; but my Friend assured me they did not *honestly* belong to him.

Henry Fielding, *The Opposition. A Vision* (1742), pp. 14–15

On the other hand, the 'huge Box' labelled 'PUBLIC SPIRIT', in which 'every Passenger [in the opposition wagon] carries his *own private Goods*', was completely 'cramm'd with *Ambition, Malice, Envy, Avarice, Disaffection, Disappointment, Pride, Revenge*, and many other heavy Commodities' (*The Opposition*, p. 16).

Fielding, then, appears at the last to have been persuaded that the opposition's outcry against Walpole was far from disinterested. Pope might not have been prepared to go that far, but he too was unable to envisage a way of dislodging the Great Man's hold on office. 'One Thousand Seven Hundred and Forty' is gloomily pessimistic about the very possibility of change for the better:

> O WRETCHED B[ritain], jealous now of all,
> What God, what mortal, shall prevent thy fall?
> Turn, turn thy eyes from wicked men in place,
> And see what succour from the Patriot Race.

Alexander Pope, Works (1797), IV, 353

It was in this state of mind, clearly, that the fourth book of *The Dunciad* was written, 'to declare the *Completion* of the *Prophecies* mention'd at the end' of Book III of the earlier version. In *The New Dunciad*, the vision of 'Universal Darkness' proclaimed in *The Dunciad Variorum* of 1729 is no longer merely a vision as far as Pope is concerned. With the restoration of the (allegorical) Kingdom of Dulness, it has become an established fact:

> 'Twas when the Dog-star's unpropitious ray
> Smote ev'ry Brain, and wither'd ev'ry Bay;
> Sick was the Sun, the Owl forsook his bow'r,
> The moon-struck Prophet felt the madding hour:
> Then rose the Seed of Chaos, and of Night,
> To blot out Order, and extinguish Light,
> Of dull and venal a new World to mold,
> And bring Saturnian days of Lead and Gold.
> She mounts the Throne: her head a Cloud conceal'd,
> In broad Effulgence all below reveal'd,
> ('Tis thus aspiring Dulness ever shines,)
> Soft on her lap her Laureat son reclines.
> Beneath her footstool, Science groans in Chains,
> And Wit dreads Exile, Penalties and Pains.
> There foam'd rebellious Logic, gagg'd and bound,
> There, stript, fair Rhet'ric languish'd on the ground,
> His blunted Arms by Sophistry are born,
> And shameless Billinsgate her Robes adorn.
> Morality, by her false Guardians drawn,
> Chicane in Furs, and Casuistry in Lawn,
> Gasps, as they straiten at each end the Cord,
> And dies, when Dulness gives her Page the word.

Alexander Pope, The New Dunciad (1724), pp.2–4

The New Dunciad appeared in March 1742 – over a month after Walpole had resigned on 1 February 1742. In the event, the cynicism of *The Opposition. A Vision* had proved to be unfounded, as the opposition message that foreign policy was being mishandled finally seems to have convinced a sufficiently large number of independent MPs. 'The general election of 1741 was the beginning of the end for Walpole', W. A. Speck observes. Although 'the ministry survived the polls with a slight majority [. . .] it was a government divided against itself' (*Stability and Strife* (1977), pp. 235, 237). As mentioned earlier, the deciding factor appears to have been its failure to secure the chairmanship of the crucially important Committee of Privileges and Elections, which decided disputed election results – usually in the government's favour! With his keen political vision Walpole saw the writing on the wall and the apparently unassailable Robinocracy was suddenly at an end.

Epilogue: The Forty-Five

Alas! on one alone our all relies,
Let him be honest, and he must be wise,
Let him no trifler from his   school, [*sic*]
Nor like his   still a   [*sic*]
Be but a man! unminister'd, alone,
And free at once the Senate and the Throne;
Esteem the public love his best supply,
A [son's?] true glory his integrity;
Rich *with* his   *in*   his strong, [*sic*]
Affect no conquest, but endure no wrong.
Whatever his religion or his blood,
His public virtue makes his title good.
Europe's just balance and our own may stand,
And one man's honesty redeem the land.

Alexander Pope, 'One Thousand Seven Hundred and Forty'
Works (1797), IV, 356

In a sense, Walpole's fall indicated that the future relationship between Crown and Parliament, which had been left in the balance in the Revolution Settlement itself, was still being worked out over half a century after 1688. At the heart of his decision to resign was his awareness of the growing importance of the House of Commons. He had not lost the support of the King. Far from it. George II wished him to carry on. But Walpole could no longer rely on a majority in the House of Commons. And without the support of the Commons Walpole could not do the King's business.

George II promoted Walpole to the House of Lords as Earl of Orford and attempted to shore up the 'Old Corps' of Court Whigs led by Henry Pelham (who, from 1743 onwards, was in effect the King's Prime Minister) with reinforcements under Carteret and Pulteney, politicians derided by Pope in 'One Thousand Seven Hundred and Forty' under the all-embracing label of 'the Patriot Race':

C[arteret], his own proud dupe, thinks Monarchs things
Made just for him, as other fools for Kings;
Controls, decides, insults thee [Britain] every hour,
And antedates the hatred due to Pow'r.
    Thro' Clouds of Passion P[ulteney]'s views are clear,
He foams a Patriot to subside a Peer;
Impatient sees his country bought and sold,
And damns the market where he takes no gold.

Alexander Pope, *Works* (1797), IV, 353

Unwilling or unable to recognise that power was inexorably
shifting away from the Crown to the House of Commons, Pope
looked not to patriot politicians in Parliament to save 'wretched
Britain' but to a 'Patriot King'. He was not alone in offering this
anachronistic analysis of the political situation. Many of Bolingbroke's essays in *The Craftsman* had harped on such a theme.
Pope and his circle retained the old-fashioned belief that a
virtuous prince ruling in his own right, 'unminister'd', not relying
on someone like Walpole, could yet 'redeem the land'.

But who was to be cast in the role of the Patriot King?
Opposition hopes had increasingly centred on Frederick, Prince
of Wales, from the time he quarrelled with his father in 1737
onwards. It is usually thought that Pope's cryptic lines at the
conclusion of 'One Thousand Seven Hundred and Forty' –
cryptic because there were evidently a number of hiatuses in the
'rough draft' from which Joseph Warton, Pope's editor, was
working – refer to Frederick. Others have tried to wring
evidence of Pope's Jacobite sympathies out of them, however:

> Whatever his religion or his blood,
> His public virtue makes his title good.

This couplet is indeed ambiguous. Perhaps Pope, after all, is
calling upon James Stuart, the Old Pretender, to 'free at once the
Senate and the Throne'. No wonder, then, that Pope 'left many
blanks for fear of the Argus Eye of those who, if they cannot
find, can fabricate treason' (Warton, *Works*, IV, [351]).

Like the relationship between Crown and Parliament which
was being painfully worked out in the extended aftermath of the

Revolution of 1688, the question of the succession itself had not yet been settled once and for all. Neither the Stuarts nor their supporters had entirely given up hopes of a Jacobite restoration. It is ironic that, although the Jacobite card had been played by Walpole many times during his long tenure of office, often rather disingenuously, it was only after his fall that Britain actually was invaded by a Jacobite force under the leadership of Charles Stuart, the Pretender's elder son.

For most of his premiership Walpole had managed to prevent Britain from becoming involved in a costly war. Not until the so-called War of Jenkins' Ear broke out late in 1739 had he been forced to give in to the clamour of those hawks who demanded that Spain should be forced to pay for their suspension of the Asiento, the contract to supply slaves to the Spanish colonies won by the British at the Treaty of Utrecht. At the end of 1740, however, 'one of the most complex conflicts of modern history, the War of the Austrian Succession' (Speck, *The Butcher* (1981), p. 14), began on the continent over the claim of the late Emperor's daughter, Maria Theresa, to the Austrian throne. Britain had treaty obligations to support Maria Theresa's claim. In addition to a sea war which he did not want, Walpole faced the prospect of an expensive entanglement on land.

Foreign policy had no little bearing on George II's choice of ministers after Walpole's fall. The King needed the support of those who would protect Hanoverian interests during the War of the Austrian Succession, and so he plumped for Carteret. But the mere thought of a land war was unpopular at home, and it was therefore difficult to persuade Parliament to vote supplies. The international situation took a turn for the worse, however, after Carteret negotiated the Treaty of Worms between Britain, Austria and Sardinia. Angered by these diplomatic moves, the French assumed the initiative. Suddenly the Jacobite threat which Walpole had harped on and on about for years became much more tangible. French support for the Pretender's cause could be taken for granted and extensive preparations for a Jacobite invasion of Britain were soon in train.

That this did not take place in 1744 was due to the intervention of bad weather, which severely damaged the British and French fleets ready to engage in the Channel and destroyed the transports intended to convoy the Jacobite army to the British mainland. France declared war on Britain, Hanover and Austria nevertheless, invading the Austrian Netherlands and defeating the allies at Fontenoy in May. It was this setback which prompted Thomson's apostrophe (added to the 1744 edition of *The Seasons*) to the retired soldier-politician, Lord Cobham, who had recently resigned his regiment as a result of his disagreement with the policies of the Pelhams:

> What pity, COBHAM, thou thy verdant Files
> Of order'd Trees shouldst here inglorious range,
> Instead of Squadrons flaming o'er the Field,
> And long-embattled Hosts! When the proud Foe
> The faithless vain Disturber of Mankind,
> Insulting *Gaul*, has roused the World to War;
> When keen, once more, within their Bounds to press
> Those polish'd Robbers, those ambitious Slaves,
> The BRITISH YOUTH would hail thy wise Command,
> Thy temper'd ardor and thy veteran Skill.

James Thomson, The Seasons (1744), p. 177

Given these early successes, it was clear that France would back another invasion attempt in the hopes of reducing the strength of British forces on the continent. On 23 July 1745 Charles Stuart landed successfully on the island of Eriskay in the Outer Hebrides. As the seven hundred men who started out with him from France had, however, been forced to turn back, it was before perhaps as few as a thousand supporters that Bonnie Prince Charlie raised his standard on 19 August. He entered an undefended Edinburgh on 17 September, nonetheless, and defeated the King's forces at Prestonpans four days later. Early in November he left Edinburgh to march on England. By 4 December he had got as far as Derby and panic gripped the country.

Charles got no further than Derby before being forced to retreat and the Jacobite rebellion was finally and brutally crushed at the Battle of Culloden in April 1746. The state of affairs in the autumn of 1745 was sufficiently alarming, however, for Fielding to pen a number of pamphlets and periodical essays, including *A Serious Address To the People of Great Britain*, which sought to remind his countrymen of the threat posed by the Pretender to the British constitution:

> The Rebellion lately begun in *Scotland*, under the Banner of *a popish Pretender*, encourag'd and assisted with the Counsels and Arms of *France* and *Spain*, is no longer an Object of your Derision. The Progress of these Rebels is such, as should awaken your Apprehensions at least, and no longer suffer you to neglect the proper Methods for your Defence. The Cause, indeed, is of such a Nature, that the *least* Danger is sufficient to *alarm* us; but the *highest* (was it possible to arrive at such an Height) should not *dishearten* or *terrify* us from engaging in it.
>
> I am unwilling to think there is a Man in this Kingdom, Papists excepted, *weak* enough to wish well to this Rebellion. I am as unwilling to believe there is one, who desires to preserve our present Constitution, *base* enough to decline the Hazard of his Life, and of his Fortune, in its Preservation. Is any *Englishman* so ignorant, as not to know the Happiness of our present Constitution? So insensible, as not to perceive the total Destruction with which it is threatned? Or *so mean, so inglorious a Coward,* as patiently to submit to this Destruction?
>
> To what Opinion, or to what Principle, must any Man sacrifice himself and his Country, who inclines to the Pretender's Side on this Occasion? The old, obsolete, absurd Doctrine of Hereditary Right, if admitted, would not justify him: The Right of his present Majesty is much stronger and clearer, even in this Light. The suspicious Birth of the Pretender was attended with such glaring Evidence of Fraud and Imposture, that no Jury would have suffered him to have succeeded, even to a private Right descended from *James* the Second, could his Pretensions have been fairly and impartially tried before them. I shall not, however, insist upon this Point. The Doctrine itself of such an indefeasible Right to the Crown hath been justly exploded; the Legislature of the Kingdom have unanimously declared against any such Principle: The Reverse of it is Law, a Law as firmly established as any other in this Kingdom; nay, it is the Foundation, the Corner-Stone of all our Laws, and of

this Constitution itself; nor is the Declaration and Con-
firmation of this great Right of the People one of the
least of those Blessings, which we owe to the Revolution. Whatever, therefore, tends to the Shaking of this
fundamental Right, doth of itself introduce an opposite
System of Government, and *changes not only the King, but
the Constitution.*

Admitting, therefore, this Pretender to be the Son of
James the Second, the stronger is the Reason for rejecting
him. *Shall we return like a Dog to his Vomit?* Shall we bring
back that Family which we have expelled, together with
the Principles *for which* we expelled them; and Shall we
pronounce, as this insolent Man hath dared to do in his
Declaration, *that we have been under an Usurpation these fifty
Years?* That Lords and Commons, and the whole *English*
Nation, have been Traitors so long? That the Bill of
Rights, the Act of Succession, and the Act of Union,
were *High-Treason?*

Let us look back to the History of that Prince, from
whom this Pretender claims. It was not only the Difference of his Religion from that of this Country, which
made him unfit to be King of it; he was unfit to govern
even a Catholic Country, which had Liberties to defend,
because his Mind was strongly tainted with all the
Notions of absolute Power. Passive Obedience, and
Non-resistance on the Part of the Subject, and a *dispens-
ing Power* in the Crown, with an indefeasible Hereditary
Right, *Jure Divino*, were as much Articles of his political
Creed, as the Supremacy of the Pope, or Transubstantia-
tion, were of his religious one: Upon the former he acted
thro' his whole Reign [. . . .]

Henry Fielding, *A Serious Address To the People of Great Britain*
(1745), pp. 1–4

What is particularly fascinating about the arguments adduced by
Fielding in *Serious Address To the People of Great Britain* is their
similarity to those put forward by writers like Marvell in the
1670s. That they still had currency in the 1740s was largely due
to the fact that, however firmly established the Hanoverian
regime appeared to be, until the Jacobite threat was finally at an

end, the solutions that had been worked out to the political questions posed during the Exclusion Crisis and the Revolution of 1688 remained merely provisional.

Interestingly, Fielding commemorated the events of 1745 not only in political pamphlets and periodical essays, but in his masterpiece, *Tom Jones*. Although published in 1749, Fielding's novel is set at the time of the Jacobite invasion. As a consequence of Blifil's false and malicious account of his conduct, Tom is expelled by Allworthy from Paradise Hall just as Bonnie Prince Charlie's army is marching south 'into *England*, intending, as it was thought, to fight the King's Forces, and to attempt pushing forward to the Metropolis' (*Tom Jones*, III, 85). '*Jones* had some Heroic Ingredients in his Composition', we are told, 'and was a hearty Well-wisher to the glorious Cause of Liberty, and of the Protestant Religion'. Coming across a company of soldiers marching north to encounter the Jacobite army, and 'think[ing] no Man can engage in a nobler Cause than that of his Religion', Tom decides to serve as a volunteer (*Tom Jones*, III, 95).

What was Fielding's purpose in making Tom's adventures on the road coincide with the Forty-Five rebellion? Sets of characters in Fielding's novel are distinguished among other things by their political attitudes. Western is a supporter of 'the Country interest', and a Jacobite sympathiser on the quiet. So is Partridge. Squire Allworthy, on the other hand, is a staunch Hanoverian like Tom. By locating the action of *Tom Jones* at the time of the Jacobite invasion Fielding gives himself the opportunity to address ideological issues at the heart of his novel. Some critics, indeed, view *Tom Jones* as an allegory of the constitutional condition of post-Revolution Britain itself.

Perhaps the best episode to use to illustrate the way in which *Tom Jones* might be said to be a vehicle for the consideration of political matters occurs two-thirds of the way through the novel. On the road to Coventry Jones and Partridge encounter 'a Company of *Egyptians*, or as they are vulgarly called *Gypsies*':

> It is impossible to conceive a happier Set of People than appeared here to be met together. The utmost Mirth indeed shewed itself in every Countenance; nor was their Ball totally void of all Order and Decorum. Perhaps it had more than a Country Assembly is sometimes conducted with: For these People are subject to a formal

> Government and Laws of their own, and all pay Obedi-
> ence to one great Magistrate whom they call their King.
>
> Henry Fielding, *Tom Jones* (1749), IV, 283–4

As we have seen, rival versions of kingship were very much on
the minds of Britons during the Forty-Five. Like Marvell in *An
Account Of the Growth of Popery, And Arbitrary Government in England*
seventy years earlier, those who opposed a Jacobite restoration
represented it as a threat to liberty and property because it would
result in arbitrary monarchy rather than the limited monarchy
confirmed by the Revolution of 1688. Charles Stuart was so well
aware of this stock response to Jacobitism that he issued a
number of proclamations criticising the Hanoverian regime along
the lines made familiar by the opposition during the long years
of Walpole's premiership. Little wonder, then, that Fielding's
portrait of the boorish, ignorant Squire Western, which owed so
much to Addison's description of the Fox-hunter, firmly linked
'the Country-interest' with Jacobitism, in contradistinction to
what Western calls Mrs Western's '*Hanoverian* gibberish'.

The King of the Gypsies proves to be a wise and merciful
ruler, however. Having witnessed an example of his justice

> *Jones* afterwards proceeded very gravely to sing forth the
> Happiness of those Subjects who lived under such a
> Magistrate.
>
> Indeed their Happiness appears to have been so
> compleat, that we are aware lest some Advocate for
> arbitrary Power should hereafter quote the Case of those
> People, as an Instance of the great Advantages which
> attend that Government above all others.
>
> And here we will make a Concession, which would not
> perhaps have been expected from us, That no limited
> Form of Government is capable of rising to the same
> Degree of Perfection, or of producing the same Benefits
> to Society with this. Mankind have never been so happy,
> as when the greatest Part of the then known World was
> under the Dominion of a single Master; and this State of
> their Felicity continued during the Reigns of five suc-
> cessive Princes. This was the true Æra of the Golden
> Age, and the only Golden Age which ever had any

Existence, unless in the warm Imaginations of the Poets, from the Expulsion from *Eden* down to this day.

In reality, I know but of one solid Objection to absolute Monarchy. The only Defect in which excellent Constitution seems to be the Difficulty of finding any Man adequate to the Office of an absolute Monarch: For this indispensably requires three Qualities very difficult, as it appears from History, to be found in princely Natures: First, a sufficient Quantity of Moderation in the Prince, to be contented with all the Power which is possible for him to have. 2dly, Enough of Wisdom to know his own Happiness. And, 3rdly, Goodness sufficient to support the Happiness of others, when not only compatible with, but instrumental to his own.

Now if an absolute Monarch with all these great and rare Qualifications should be allowed capable of conferring the greatest Good on Society, it must be surely granted, on the contrary, that absolute Power vested in the Hands of one who is deficient in them all, is likely to be attended with no less a Degree of Evil.

In short our own Religion furnishes us with adequate ideas of the Blessing, as well as Curse which may attend absolute Power. The Pictures of Heaven and Hell will place a very lively Image of both before our Eyes: For though the Prince of the latter can have no Power, but what he originally derives from the omnipotent Sovereign in the former; yet it plainly appears from Scripture, that absolute Power in his infernal Dominions is granted to their Diabolical Ruler. This is indeed the only absolute Power which can by Scripture be derived from Heaven. If therefore the several Tyrannies upon Earth can prove any Title to a divine Authority, it must be derived from this original grant to the Prince of Darkness, and these subordinate Deputations must consequently come immediately from him whose Stamp they so expressly bear.

To conclude, as the Examples of all Ages shew us that Mankind in general desire Power only to do Harm, and when they obtain it, use it for no other Purpose; it is not consonant with even the least Degree of Prudence to hazard an Alternative, where our Hopes are poorly kept in Countenance by only two or three Exceptions out of a thousand Instances to alarm our Fears. In this Case it will be much wiser to submit to a few Inconveniences arising from the dispassionate Deafness of Laws, than to remedy them by applying to the passionate open Ears of a Tyrant.

Nor can the Examples of the *Gypsies*, tho' possibly they may have long been happy under this Form of Government, be here urged; since we must remember the very material Respect in which they differ from all other People, and to which perhaps this their Happiness is entirely owing, namely, that they have no false Honours among them; and that they look on Shame as the most grievous Punishment in the World.

Henry Fielding, *Tom Jones* (1749), IV, 291–5

The lesson Fielding wishes his readers to learn from this episode is readily apparent: however much one might carp at certain aspects of the Hanoverian regime, people are much safer and happier when they live under the auspices of limited, rather than absolute, monarchy.

As late as 1749, then, the question of the succession was still being debated not only in writings of an openly political nature, but in works of the creative imagination. *Tom Jones* is the vehicle for the discussion of a range of ideological issues, most of which had been current in 1678 also. When, for instance, right at the end of the book, Squire Western is trying to persuade his daughter, Sophia, that she should marry Tom, he makes use of an argument which might readily have come out of the chapter on obedience in *The Whole Duty of Man*, a work Fielding cites by name in *Joseph Andrews*. 'Tell her I'm her Father', says Western, 'and of the horrid Sin of Disobedience, and of the dreadful Punishment of it in t'other World' (*Tom Jones*, VI, 228).

The relationship between Fielding's openly political writings on the Forty-Five and his fictional reconstruction of the events of the year of the rebellion in *Tom Jones* is characteristic of late seventeenth- and early-eighteenth-century English literature. Many of the most prominent writers of the period were actively involved in writing pamphlets and periodical essays which were overtly political. At the same time many of the most significant works of literature of the period had unmistakable political overtones.

This was because Augustan satirists were generally committed to a political view of the world and engaged in the production of *public*, rather than private, works. There was, after all, a tremendous amount at stake. From the beginning of agitation against the succession of a Popish prince to the final destruction of the Jacobite threat at Culloden the safety of the Protestant succession was at the top of the political agenda. And, as we have seen, preoccupation with the succession had a number of other consequences. It required extensive British involvement in lengthy continental wars, so that as a result financial revolution closely followed constitutional revolution. This, in turn, led to changes in the social structure.

With the traditional order under threat from new forces within society the Augustan satirists pondered the fate of the old ways. The works of Swift, Pope and Gay – the Scriblerian satirists – best express the hopes and fears of those social conservatives who resented change. Interestingly, the fall of Walpole coincided, to all intents and purposes, with the demise of this generation of writers. Gay had died during the 1730s, but the ailing Pope finally succumbed in 1744, to be followed by Swift during the Forty-Five itself. Fielding was not destined to survive them long. Worn out through ill-health, he died in 1754.

Although Fielding's literary and political inclinations suggest an ideological perspective not far removed from those of the Scriblerians, he was of a younger generation, born in 1707, the same year as Samuel Johnson, the figure who was to dominate the literary scene during the second half of the eighteenth century. By 1750, then, it was not only the political landscape which was significantly different. Changes in literary taste were also taking place. The emergence of a cult of sensibility was ushering in a new era, one dominated by sentiment rather than satire. Writers like Sterne and Goldsmith sometimes worked within this new idiom for satiric effect, but increasingly those voices still raised in protest about the passing of the old order sound increasingly out of tune.

Notes

1. I.e., a Roman Catholic.
2. Roberto Francesco Romulo Bellarmine or Bellarmino (1542–1621), the Italian theologian and Roman Catholic apologist. He was one of the leaders of the Moderns in Swift's *Battel of the Books.*
3. As Page of his Majesty's Bedchamber and Keeper of the King's Private Closet, William Chiffinch (1602?–1688) was in a perfect position to act as Charles II's pimp in the manner described in this poem.
4. Robert Spencer, second Earl of Sunderland (1641–1702), was Lord President of the Council under James II, the King's confidante, and in effect chief minister. As a result he was associated with the worst excesses of James' policies, and was therefore sacrificed in a vain attempt to stem the tide of public opinion. Despite his expedient conversion to Roman Catholicism, he managed to survive the Revolution to perform a similar function for William III for a time as Lord Chamberlain.
5. The words in bold were made emphatic in the original edition of the text by being printed in black Gothic letters.
6. The Fox-hunter is explicitly comparing the Whig-dominated House of Commons with the Rump which was left after Pride's Purge during the Civil War.
7. Sir Edward Coke (1552–1634), the judge and legal authority.
8. Allen, first Earl Bathurst (1684–1775) was not only the friend and correspondent of Swift and Pope, but the addressee of Pope's *Epistle to Bathurst.*

Chronological Table

Date	Contemporary events	Notable literary and publishing events
1678	Popish Plot; start of Exclusion Crisis	Marvell, *Account of the Growth of Popery*; Bunyan, *The Pilgrim's Progress*
1681	Shaftesbury's trial	Dryden, *Absalom and Achitophel*; Marvell, *Miscellaneous Poems*
1682		Otway, *Venice Preserved*
1683	Rye-House Plot	
1685	Accession of James II; Monmouth Rebellion	
1688	Glorious Revolution; flight of James II	
1689	Convention Parliament; Declaration of Rights; accession of William III and Mary II	Locke, *Two Treatises of Government*
1690		Locke, *An Essay concerning Humane Understanding*
1694	Death of Mary II; founding of Bank of England	Molesworth, *An Account of Denmark*
1695	End of pre-publication censorship in England with the expiry of Licensing Act	Locke, *The Reasonableness of Christianity*

Date	Contemporary events	Notable literary and publishing events
1696		Toland, *Christianity Not Mysterious*
1697	Treaty of Ryswick; standing army controversy	
1698	First Partition Treaty	
1700	Second Partition Treaty; death of Charles II of Spain	Defoe, *True-Born Englishman*; Congreve, *Way of the World*
1701	Act of Settlement; Grand Alliance; death of James II	
1702	Death of William III; accession of Queen Anne; England enters War of Spanish Succession	Defoe, *Shortest Way with the Dissenters*
1704	Battle of Blenheim	Swift, *A Tale of a Tub*; Defoe, *Review*
1706	Battle of Ramellies	Farquhar, *The Recruiting Officer*
1707	Act of Union	Farquhar, *The Beaux' Stratagem*
1709	Battle of Malplaquet; Copyright Act	Steele, *Tatler*; Sacheverell, *The Perils Of False Brethren*
1710	Trial of Sacheverell; Ministerial Revolution	Swift, *Examiner*

Date	Contemporary events	Notable literary and publishing events
1711		Addison and Steele, *Spectator*; Swift, *Conduct of the Allies*
1712		Pope, *The Rape of the Lock*
1713	Treaty of Utrecht	Pope, *Windsor-Forest*; Addison, *Cato*
1714	Death of Queen Anne	Pope, *The Rape of the Lock* (five-canto version); Mandeville, *Fable of the Bees*
1715	Jacobite rebellion	Addison, *Free-Holder*
1719		Defoe, *Robinson Crusoe*
1720	South Sea Bubble	
1722		Defoe, *Moll Flanders*
1723	Atterbury trial	Mandeville, *Fable of the Bees* (revised)
1724		Swift, *Drapier's Letters*; Defoe, *Roxana*; *Tour thro' the Whole Island of Great Britain*
1726		Swift, *Gulliver's Travels*; *The Craftsman*; Thomson, *Winter*
1727	Death of George I; accession of George II	
1728		Gay, *The Beggar's Opera*; Pope, *The Dunciad*
1729		Pope, *The Dunciad Variorum*; Swift, *A Modest Proposal*
1730		Thomson, *The Seasons*

Date	Contemporary events	Notable literary and publishing events
1731		Pope, *Epistle to Burlington*
1733	Excise Crisis	Pope, *Essay on Man*, Part I; Swift, *On Poetry: A Rapsody*
1735		Thomson, *Liberty*
1737	Theatrical Licensing Act	Pope, *Epistle to Augustus*; Fielding, *Historical Register*, *Common Sense*
1740		Richardson, *Pamela*
1742	Fall of Walpole	Fielding, *The Opposition. A Vision*; Pope, *The New Dunciad*
1743		Pope, *The Dunciad, In Four Books*; Fielding, *Miscellanies*; *Jonathan Wild*
1744	Britain enters War of Austrian Succession	
1745	Forty-Five Rebellion	
1748	End of War of Austrian Succession	Richardson, *Clarissa*; Smollett, *Roderick Random*; Cleland, *Memoirs of a Woman of Pleasure*
1749		Fielding, *Tom Jones*; Johnson, *Vanity of Human Wishes*
1750		Johnson, *The Rambler*

Bibliography

Place of publication is London unless stated otherwise.

PRIMARY SOURCES

Addison, Joseph, *Cato* (1713)
— *The Free-Holder, Or Political Essays* (1716)
Allestree, Richard, *The Whole Duty of Man* (1659)
Bohun, Edmund, *The History of the Desertion* (1689)
Burnet, Gilbert, *A History of My Own Time* (Oxford, 1833)
— *A Pastoral Letter* (1689)
The Champion (1741)
Common Sense: Or, The Englishman's Journal (1738)
The Craftsman: Or, the Countryman's Journal (1726–51)
Defoe, Daniel, *The Legion-Letter* (1701)
— *The Mock Mourners: A Satyr by Way of Elegy on King William* (1702)
— *Moll Flanders* (1722)
— *A New Satyr on the Parliament* (1701)
— *The Review* (1704–13)
— *The Shortest Way with the Dissenters* (1702, 1703)
— *The True-Born Englishman: A Satyr* (1700)
Dryden, John, *Absalom and Achitophel* (1681)
— *Mac Flecknoe* (1682)
Fielding, Henry, *The Historical Register for the Year 1736* (1737)
— *Miscellanies* (1743)
— *The Opposition. A Vision* (1742)
— *A Serious Address To the People of Great Britain* (1745)
— *Tom Jones* (1749)
Filmer, Sir Robert, *Observations upon Aristotle's Politiques* (1652)
— *Patriarcha: or the Natural Power of Kings* (1680)
Free Briton (1732)
Gay, John, *The Beggar's Opera* (1728)
Harrington, James, *The Common-Wealth of Oceana* (1656)
Hervey, John, Lord, *Some Materials Towards Memoirs of the Reign of George II*, ed. Romney Sedgwick (1931)

Hobbes, Thomas, *Leviathan* (1651)

James I, *Workes* (1616)

Johnson, Samuel, *An Argument Proving, That the Abrogation of King James [. . .] was according to the Constitution of the English Government* (1692)

Johnson, Samuel, *London* (1738)

Journals of the House of Commons

A Key, Being Observations and Explanatory Notes, upon the Travels of Lemuel Gulliver (1726)

Locke, John, *Two Treatises of Government* (1690)

Mandeville, Bernard, *The Fable of the Bees: Or, Private Vices, Publick Benefits* (1724)

Marvell, Andrew, *An Account Of the Growth of Popery, And Arbitrary Government in England* (1678)

Molesworth, Robert, *An Account of Denmark, As It was in the Year 1692* (1694)

Oldham, John, *Garnets Ghost* (1679)

Otway, Thomas *Venice Preserved, or, A Plot Discover'd* (1682)

Pope, Alexander, *The Dunciad, In Four Books* (1743)

— *The Dunciad Variorum* (1729)

— *Epistle to Augustus* (1737)

— *Epistle to Bathurst* (1733)

— *Epistle to Burlington* (1731)

— *An Essay on Man* (1733–34)

— *The New Dunciad* (1742)

— *Windsor-Forest* (1713)

— *Works*, ed. Joseph Warton (1797)

Sacheverell, Henry, *The Perils of False Brethren, both in Church, and State* (1709)

— *The Political Union* (1702)

Seller, Abednigo, *The History of Passive Obedience Since the Reformation* (1689)

Shakespeare, William, *Richard II* (1597)

Sherlock, William, *The Case of Allegiance due to Soveraign Powers, Stated and Resolved* (1691)

Shippen, William, *Faction Display'd* (1704)

Sidney, Algernon, *Discourses concerning Government* (1704)

'Sir Edmund Berry Godfrey's Ghost' (1679)

The Spectator (1711–13)

Swift, Jonathan, *An Argument against Abolishing Christianity* (1717)

— *The Bubble* (1721)

Swift, Jonathan, *The Conduct of the Allies, and of the Late Ministry, In Beginning and Carrying on the Present War* (1711)
— 'Causes of the Wretched Condition of Ireland'
— *The Correspondence of Jonathan Swift*, ed. Harold Williams (Oxford, 1963–65)
— *A Discourse of the Contests and Dissentions Between the Nobles and the Commons in Athens and Rome* (1701)
— *The Examiner* (1710–11)
— *Gulliver's Travels* (1726)
— *A Letter to the Right Honourable the Lord Viscount Molesworth* (1724)
— *On Poetry: A Rapsody* (1733)
— *A Proposal For the universal Use of Irish Manufacture* (1721)
The Tatler (1709–11)
Thomson, James, *Britannia* (1729)
— *Liberty* (1735–36)
— *The Seasons* (1744)
Toland, John, *The Art of Governing by Partys* (1701)
— *The Militia Reform'd* (1698)
Tories and Tory Principles Ruinous to both Prince and People (1714)
Trenchard, John and Thomas Gordon, *Cato's Letters* (1722)
Tutchin, John, *The Foreigners* (1700)
Wilmot, John, Earl of Rochester, *Miscellaneous Works* (1707)
— *Poems on Several Occasions* (1685)

SECONDARY SOURCES

In addition to the secondary works cited in the text, the following list includes a selection of books on late-seventeenth- and early-eighteenth-century history.

Ashcraft, Richard, *Revolutionary Politics and Locke's 'Two Treatises of Government'* (Princeton, 1986)
Black, Jeremy (ed.), *Britain in the Age of Walpole* (1984)
Booth, Wayne C., *A Rhetoric of Irony* (Chicago, 1974)
Dickinson, H.T., *Liberty and Property: Political Ideology in Eighteenth-Century Britain* (1977)
Downie, J.A., *Jonathan Swift, Political Writer* (1984)
— *Robert Harley and the Press: Propaganda and Public Opinion in the Age of Swift and Defoe* (Cambridge, 1979)
Goldgar, Bertrand A., *Walpole and the Wits: The Relation of Politics to Literature, 1722–1742* (Lincoln, Nebraska, 1977)

Harris, Michael. *London Newspapers in the Age of Walpole: A Study in the Origins of the Modern English Press* (1987)

Harris, Tim, Paul Seaward and Mark Goldie (eds), *The Politics of Religion in Restoration England* (Oxford, 1990)

Hirsch, E.D., Jr, *Validity in Interpretation* (New Haven, 1969)

Holmes, Geoffrey (ed.), *Britain after the Glorious Revolution 1689–1714* (1969)

— *British Politics in the Age of Anne* (1967)

Hume, Robert D., 'Texts Within Contexts: Notes Toward a Historical Method', *Philological Quarterly*, 71 (1992), 69–100.

Jones, Clyve (ed.), *Britain in the First Age of Party, 1680–1750* (1987)

Jones, J.R., *Country and Court: England 1658–1714* (1978)

— *The First Whigs: The Politics of the Exclusion Crisis 1678–1683* (1961)

— (ed.), *The Restored Monarchy 1660–1688* (1979)

Kenyon, J.P., *The Popish Plot* (Harmondsworth, 1972)

— *Revolution Principles: The Politics of Party 1689–1720* (Cambridge, 1977)

Langford, Paul, *The Excise Crisis: Society and Politics in the Age of Walpole* (Oxford, 1975)

Maccubbin, Robert P. and Martha Hamilton-Phillips (eds), *The Age of William III & Mary II: Power, Politics, and Patronage 1688–1702* (Williamsburg, 1989)

Plumb, J.H., *The Growth of Political Stability in England, 1675–1725* (Oxford, 1967)

Scott, Jonathan, *Algernon Sidney and the Restoration Crisis, 1677–1683* (Cambridge, 1990)

Speck, W.A., *The Butcher: The Duke of Cumberland and the Suppression of the 45* (Oxford, 1981)

— *Reluctant Revolutionaries: Englishmen and the Revolution of 1688* (Oxford, 1988)

— *Stability and Strife: England 1714–1760* (1977)

Todorov, Tzvetan, *Mikhail Bakhtin: The Dialogical Principle*, trans. Wlad Godzich (Manchester, 1984)

Trevelyan, G.M., *England Under Queen Anne* (1930–34)

Western, J.R., *Monarchy and Revolution: The English State in the 1680s* (1972)

Index

Act of Settlement, 56–7, 58, 62, 66, 83, 84, 88, 90, 94, 151, 159
Act of Toleration, 66, 68, 69, 83
Act of Uniformity, 83
Act of Union, 76, 151, 159
Addison, Joseph, 78, 82–5, 91–4, 153, 160, *see also Spectator, The,* and *Tatler, The*
   Cato, 84–5, 160
   Free-Holder, 91–4, 153, 160
Allestree, Richard, 41, *see also Whole Duty of Man, The*
Anne, Queen, 56, 63–70, 76, 79, 87–9, 92, 159, 160
Asiento, 148
Atterbury, Francis, 111, 112, 160

Bank of England, 49, 82–4, 85, 158
Barber, Mary, 131
Bath, Earl of, *see under* Pulteney, William
Bathurst, Allen, Earl of, 127, 157
Bellarmine, Roberto Francesco Romulo, 22–3, 157
Bennett, G.V., 111
Bill of Rights, 51, 151
Blenheim, Battle of, 76, 159
Bohun, Edmund, 36–7
   History of the Desertion, The, 36–7
Bolingbroke, Henry, St John, Viscount, 90, 147
'Book of Martyrs', 6
Booth, Wayne C., 1
Bunyan, John, 158
Burlington, Richard Boyle, Earl of, 126–7, 161
Burnet, Gilbert, 5, 37, 41, 79
   Pastoral Letter, A, 37, 40

Caroline, Queen, 129, 134–5
Carteret, John, Lord, 146–7, 148

Cato's Letters, 95–6, 98
Champion, The, 141, 143
Charles I, 11, 75
Charles II, 2, 5, 6, 8, 11, 17, 18, 26–30, 55, 62, 78, 92, 157
Charles II of Spain, 58–9, 159
Chiffinch, William, 27, 157
'Church in Danger', debate over, 66–76
Cibber, Colley, 120
Cleland, John, 161
Cobham, Sir Richard Temple, Viscount, 149
Coke, Sir Edward, 122, 157
Coleman, Edward, 6
Common Sense, 133–5, 140–1, 143, 161
Congreve, William, 159
Convention Parliament, 33–4, 42, 158
Copyright Act, 159
'Country' ideology, 46–9
Craftsman, The, 115–16, 121–3, 147, 160
Culloden, Battle of, 149, 156

Declaration of Rights, 158, *see also* Bill of Rights
Defoe, Daniel, 31, 53–4, 58, 59–60, 64, 69–70, 76, 88, 102–5, 159, 160
   Legion's Memorial, 59
   Mock Mourners, The, 64
   Moll Flanders, 102–5, 160
   Review, The, 76, 159
   Robinson Crusoe, 160
   Roxana, 160
   Shortest Way with the Dissenters, The, 67–70, 159
   Tour thro' the Whole Island of Great Britain, A, 160

True-Born Englishman, The, 31, 53–4, 159
'Ye True-Born Englishmen proceed', 57–8
Democrats, 2
Dickinson, H.T., 51
Dissenters, 2, 66–70, 71
Divine Right of Kings, doctrine of, 8–9, 17, 20–6, 29–30, 33, 35, 39, 42, 44, 47, 66, 71, 74–6, 150–1
Dryden, John, xii, 5, 7, 12, 28–30, 51, 64, 78, 158
    Absalom and Achitophel, 5, 7–8, 12, 28, 29, 51, 158
    Mac Flecknoe, xii, 64
Dyer, John, 93

Elizabeth I, 8, 33
Essex, Arthur Capel, Earl of, 29
Excise Crisis, 140, 161
Exclusion Crisis, 5, 7–8, 12, 14, 29, 31, 152, 158

Farquhar, George, 159
'Festival of the Golden Rump', *see under Common Sense*
Fielding, Henry, 105–8, 109, 111, 135–40, 142–3, 149–55, 156, 161
    Historical Register for the Year 1736, The, 135–8, 142, 161
    Jonathan Wild, 138–9, 161
    Joseph Andrews, 155
    Miscellanies, 138–9, 161
    Opposition: A Vision, The, 142–3, 145, 161
    Serious Address To the People of Great Britain, A, 149–51
    Tom Jones, 105–8, 152–5, 161
Fifteen Rebellion, 91–4, 160
Filmer, Sir Robert, 21–5, 41
    Anarchy of a Limited or Mixed Monarchy, The, 21
    Observations upon Aristotle's Politiques, 21, 24
    Patriarcha, 21–4
Financial Revolution, 49–50, 96–9, 109, 111, 156

Fire of London, 7
Fontenoy, Battle of, 149
Forty-Five rebellion, 2, 149–53, 155, 156, 161
Foxe, John, 6
Frederick Louis, Prince of Wales, 129, 140, 146–7
Free-Holder, The, *see under* Addison, Joseph

Garnet, Henry, 13
Gay, John, 111, 116–18, 130, 139, 156, 160
    Beggar's Opera, The, 111, 116–18, 123, 135, 139, 160
George I, 84, 89, 90–1, 111, 115, 116, 123, 140, 160
George II, 120, 123, 126, 129, 131, 133–5, 140, 146, 148, 150, 152, 160
Glorious Revolution, *see under* Revolution of 1688
Gloucester, Duke of, 56
Godfrey, Sir Edmund Berry, 5–6, 13, 27
Golden Rump, *see under Common Sense*
Goldsmith, Oliver, 156
Gordon, Thomas, 95–6, 98, 101
Government, forms of, 3, 8–9, 17–25, 33–43, 64–5, 74–6, 110, 152–3
Grand Alliance, 61, 87, 159
Granville, Earl, *see under* Carteret, John, Lord
Gunpowder Plot, 7, 13, 74
Gwyn, Nell, 27

Halifax, George Savile, Marquis of, 11–12
Harrington, James, 48
    Oceana, 48
Hereditary Right, doctrine of, *see under* Divine Right of Kings, doctrine of
Hirsch, E.D., Jr, 1
Hobbes, Thomas, 13–14, 41, 102, 105, 107, 133
    Leviathan, 14, 107
Hume, Robert D., 17

Jacobitism, 35, 39, 62, 63, 64–6, 72, 76, 88, 90–4, 111, 147–53, 156
James I, 9
James II, 6, 27, 30, 31–40, 42, 56, 57, 61, 63, 65, 69, 150–1, 157, 158
James III, the Old Pretender, *see under* Stuart, James Francis Edward, the Old Pretender
James, Duke of York, *see under* James II
Jesuits, 5, 13, 22, 33, 73
Johnson, Samuel (d. 1703), 39–41
  Argument Proving, That the Abrogation of King James, An, 39–40
Johnson, Samuel (d. 1784), 111, 140, 156, 161
  London, 140
Jones, Inigo, 127
Jones, J.R., 7, 27, 31
Joseph Ferdinand of Bavaria, 58

Kentish Petition, 57, 59–60

Laslett, Peter, 24
Leopold of Austria, 58, 61
L'Estrange, Sir Roger, 21, 67
Liberty, 24–5, 44–7, 48, 84–5, 88, 96, 98, 99, 131–3, 152
Liberty and Property, 17, 20, 25, 44–6, 48, 49, 53, 75, 91, 121, 124, 153
Licensing Act, 135
Locke, John, 24–5, 35, 41–4, 52, 99, 158
  Reasonableness of Christianity, The, 158
  Essay concerning Humane Understanding, An, 158
  Two Treatises of Government, 24–5, 41–4, 158
Louis XIV, 26–7, 32, 49, 58, 59, 61, 63, 76, 77–8, 81, 82, 87

Malplaquet, Battle of, 76–7, 78, 159
Mandeville, Bernard, 101–2, 105, 107, 108–9, 160

Fable of the Bees, The, 101–2, 105, 108–9, 160
Mar, John Erskine, Earl of, 91
Maria Theresa of Austria, 148
Marlborough, John Churchill, Duke of, 76–82
Marvell, Andrew, 18–21, 36, 41, 151, 153, 158
  Account Of the Growth of Popery, An, 18–21, 153, 158
Mary I, 6
Mary II, 32, 35–7, 39, 56, 158
Mary of Modena, 32
Maynwaring, Arthur, 82
Medley, The, 82
Ministerial Revolution of 1710, 79, 85, 159
Molesworth, Robert, 44–7, 99, 158
  Account of Denmark, An, 44–7, 158
Monarchy, debate about, 9, 13, 17–26, 31, 33–41, 52–3, 71, 74–6, 96, 146–7, 153–5
Monmouth, James Scott, Duke of, 30, 31
Monmouth Rebellion, 30, 31, 158

Nine Years War, 49, 58

Oates, Titus, 5–7, 17
Obedience, doctrine of, 9–12, 13, 38, 40, 74–6, 91, 93–4, 155 *see also* Divine Rights of Kings, doctrine of
Occasional Conformity, 66–7, 70, 72
Oldham, John, 12–13
  Garnets Ghost, 12–13
Order, ideology of, 1, 17, 29, 109–10, 124–5, 127–8, 144
Orford, Earl of, *see under* Walpole, Sir Robert
Ormonde, James Butler, Duke of, 90
Otway, Thomas, 14–17, 158
  Venice Preserved, 14–17, 158
Oudenarde, Battle of, 76

Palladio, 127
Partition Treaties, 58–9, 159
Patriarchalism, 21–6, 41, 44

Pelham, Henry, 146, 149
Philip V of Spain, 58, 77, 78
Pope, Alexander, 50, 63, 87–9,
    109–10, 111, 118–20, 125–8,
    130, 132, 133, 141, 143–4,
    146–7, 156, 160, 161
  Dunciad, The, 118–20, 126, 144,
    160, 161
  Dunciad, Variorum, The, 131, 144,
    160
  Epistle to Augustus, 128, 129, 132,
    133, 141, 160
  Epistle to Bathurst, 50–1, 157
  Epistle to Burlington, 126–7, 128,
    131, 161
  Essay on Man, An, 1, 109–10,
    124–5, 127–8, 161
  New Dunciad, The, 144–5, 161
  'One Thousand Seven Hundred
    and Forty', 143–4, 146–7
  Rape of the Lock, The, 160
  Windsor-Forest, 63, 87–9, 128, 160
Popish Plot, 2, 5–7, 12, 13–15, 29,
    158
Portland, Hans Willem Bentinck,
    Earl of, 51–3, 59
Portsmouth, Louise de Kéroualle
    (Carwell), Duchess of, 26, 27
Pretender, Old, *see under* Stuart,
    James Francis Edward
Protestant Succession, safety of, 2,
    6, 8, 17, 52, 56, 62, 63, 71, 76,
    111, 148, 155, 156
Pulteney, William, 146–7

Ramellies, Battle of, 76, 159
Regency Act, 88
Republicans, 2
Revolution of 1688, 25, 31–9, 44,
    51, 53, 54, 55, 56, 64–5, 66,
    69, 71, 76, 88, 91, 92, 94, 97,
    102, 146, 148, 151, 152, 153,
    157, 158
Revolution Settlement, 31, 34–9, 51,
    54, 57, 61, 70, 94, 146
Richard II, 8
Richardson, Samuel, 161
Rochester, John Wilmot, Earl of,
    12, 14, 26–7, 133

*Satyr against Reason and Mankind,
    A*, 12, 14
Satyr on Charles II, A, 26–7
Russell, William, Lord, 29
Rye House Plot, 29, 158
Ryswick, Treaty of, 49, 62, 159

Sacheverell, Henry, 66–7, 74–6, 78,
    159
  Perils of False Brethren, The, 74–6,
    159
  Political Union, The, 66–7
St John, Henry, *see under*
    Bolingbroke, Henry St John,
    Viscount
Sancroft, William, 35
Scott, Sir Walter, 7
Scriblerian satirists, 111–21, 123–31,
    156
Seller, Abednigo, 9
Sensibility, 156
Septennial Act, 94
Shaftesbury, Anthony Ashley
    Cooper, 1st Earl of, 7–8, 12,
    15, 29, 51, 158
Shaftesbury, Anthony Ashley
    Cooper, 3rd Earl of, 107–9
Shakespeare, William, 8, 20
Sherlock, William, 38–9, 41, 44
  *Case of Allegiance due to Soveraign
    Powers, The*, 38–9, 44
Shippen, William, 65
Sidney, Algernon, 3, 24, 29, 99, 132
  Discourses concerning Government, 3,
    24
Smollett, Tobias, 161
Society, structure of, 3, 12, 47–9,
    99–102, 111–12, 121, 156
Sophia, Princess, of Hanover, 65
South Sea Bubble, 96–9, 109, 111
Speck, W.A., 145, 148
Spectator, The, 82–4, 85, 160
Standing Army Controversy, 51, 55,
    95, 159
Steele, Sir Richard, 159, 160, *see also
    Spectator, The*, and *Tatler, The*
Sterne, Laurence, 156
Stuart, Charles Edward, the Young
    Pretender, 148, 149, 152, 153

Stuart, James Francis Edward, the
    Old Pretender, 2, 32, 62, 71–2,
    76, 84, 88, 90, 91–4, 146–7,
    150–1
Succession, *see under* Protestant
    Succession
Sunderland, Robert Spencer, 2nd
    Earl of, 31, 157
Swift, Jonathan, 2–3, 34–5, 45, 48,
    49–50, 60–1, 65, 70–4, 79–82,
    85–7, 97–101, 106, 111,
    112–15, 116, 117–18, 124–5,
    129–31, 135, 156, 157, 159,
    160, 161
    *Argument against Abolishing
        Christianity, An*, 72–4, 85
    Bubble, The, 97–8
    'Causes of the Wretched
        Condition of Ireland, The',
        100–1
    Conduct of the Allies, The, 85–7, 160
    'Directions for a Birth-day Song',
        130
    *Discourse of the Contests and
        Dissentions, A*, 60–1
    Examiner, The, 2–3, 34–5, 49–50,
        65, 71–2, 79–82, 159
    Gulliver's Travels, 45, 98–9,
        112–15, 124–5, 135, 160
    *Letter to the Right Honourable the
        Lord Viscount Molesworth, A*, 99
    Modest Proposal, A, 160
    On Poetry: A Rapsody, 129–31, 161
    *Proposal For the Universal Use of
        Irish Manufacture, A*, 100
    Tale of a Tub, A, 159

Tatler, The, 3, 77–8, 159
Test and Corporation Acts, 31, 66,
    72–4
Theatrical Licensing Act, 135, 161
Theobald, Lewis, 120
Thomson, James, 90, 111, 131–3,
    149, 160, 161
    Britannia, 131–2
    Liberty, 90, 132–3, 161
    Seasons, The, 132, 149, 160, 161
Toland, John, 34, 48–9, 55, 62, 159

Art of Governing by Partys, The, 55,
    62
Christianity Not Mysterious, 159
Militia Reform'd, The, 34, 48–9
Tories, 2–3, 7, 29, 35, 39, 55, 62,
    65, 71–2, 76, 77, 85, 86, 88–9,
    90, 94, 95–6
*Tories and Tory Principles Ruinous to
    both Prince and People*, 7
Townshend, Charles, Viscount, 118
Trenchard, John, 95–6, 98, 99, 101
Trevelyan, G.M., 78
Triennial Act, 94
Tutchin, John, 51–3, 54
    Foreigners, The, 51–3
Tyrrell, James, 24

Utrecht, Peace of, 87, 88, 89, 148,
    160

Virgil, 87
Vitruvius, 127

Walpole, Sir Robert, 110–45, 146,
    147, 148, 153, 156, 161
War of Jenkins' Ear, 148
War of the Austrian Succession,
    148–9, 161
War of the Spanish Succession, 64,
    76, 159
Warton, Joseph, 147
Whigs, 2–3, 7, 29, 35, 39, 54–5, 60,
    62, 64, 65, 71–2, 76, 77, 85,
    86, 90, 94–6, 99–101, 146, 157
Whole Duty of Man, The, 3, 9–11, 38,
    91, 155
Wild, Jonathan, 139–40
William III, 32, 34, 35–9, 41–2, 49,
    51, 52, 54, 55–6, 58, 62, 63,
    64–5, 67, 74, 88, 91, 93, 95,
    158, 159
William of Orange, *see under* William
    III
Worms, Treaty of, 148

York, James, Duke of, *see under*
    James II
Young, Edward, 130